THE CENTERS OF CIVILIZATION SERIES

(*For complete list see page 182*)

Chicago

BY EDWARD WAGENKNECHT

I adore Chicago. It is the pulse of America.
—SARAH BERNHARDT

UNIVERSITY OF OKLAHOMA PRESS : NORMAN

By Edward Wagenknecht

Cavalcade of the English Novel (New York, 1943)

Cavalcade of the American Novel (New York, 1952)

The Seven Worlds of Theodore Roosevelt (New York, 1958)

Nathaniel Hawthorne, Man and Writer (New York, 1961)

Mark Twain, The Man and His Work (New Edition, Norman, 1961)

Washington Irving: Moderation Displayed (New York, 1962)

The Movies in the Age of Innocence (Norman, 1962)

Edgar Allan Poe: The Man Behind the Legend (New York, 1963)

Chicago (Norman, 1964), etc., etc.

Library of Congress Catalog Card Number 64-11322

Copyright 1964 by the University of Oklahoma Press,
Publishing Division of the University.
Composed and printed at Norman, Oklahoma, U.S.A.,
by the University of Oklahoma Press.
First Edition.

For Ellen Van Volkenburg,
distinguished artist and dear friend, who, in the days of
the Little Theater, contributed much
to civilization in Chicago

Note

The Author is very grateful to the outstanding authority on Chicago, Professor Bessie Louise Pierce, who, at his request, very kindly read and criticized his manuscript.

The chapter on Jane Addams was written, in its original form, during her lifetime and read by her.

Thanks are expressed also to the Art Institute of Chicago, the Chicago Natural History Museum, the Museum of Science and Industry, and the Lyric Opera, all of whom sent useful materials for this book, and to my son, Robert Edward Wagenknecht, for assistance in proofreading.

EDWARD WAGENKNECHT

Contents

Chicago

I

The White City

"CENTER OF CIVILIZATION"?— Chicago? The city of Al Capone and "Big Bill" Thompson ("Throw away your hammer and get a horn")? The "Hog Butcher for the World"? The city which achieved a great World's Fair and murdered the mayor at the end of it? which welcomed an archbishop to his new diocese at a civic dinner where a crazy chef put arsenic in his soup? Even so.

There is no use trying to be neutral about Chicago or the land which she inhabits. Nobody ever has been. "I landed," wrote the pioneer Gurdon S. Hubbard, "and climbing a tree, gazed in admiration on the first prairie I had ever seen. The waving grass, intermingling with a rich profusion of wild flowers, was the most beautiful sight I had ever gazed upon." In 1870 Thomas Hughes found her "the wonder of the wonderful West," and Bismarck longed to visit America "if only to see that Chicago."

For a very different impression, listen to Fredrika Bremer in 1863: "Chicago is one of the most miserable and ugly cities which I have yet seen in America, and is very little deserving of its name, 'Queen of the Lake'; for, sitting there on the shore of the lake in wretched dishabille, she resembles rather a huckstress than a queen." "Chicago," said Emerson, "grows so fast that one ceases to respect civic growth." Kipling, in 1906, is so intemperate as to exclude himself from serious consideration: "Having seen it, I urgently desire never to see it again. It is inhabited by savages. Its water is the water of the Hughli, and its air is dirt." But what are we to say of Don Marquis in 1932? "Nobody can think of Chicago as actually existing; a person would go mad if he did; it is a grotesque nightmare and easily recognizable as such."

Early observers could not even agree that Chicago had a future. While Schoolcraft saw her as "a great thoroughfare for strangers, merchants, and travelers," the most William H. Keating could grant was that "at some distant day" she might be a port between the Great Lakes and the Mississippi. Milwaukee, Michigan City, and Galena were all, at different times, rated ahead of her, and oddly enough it was Jefferson Davis, who, as army engineer, insisted that the mouth of the Chicago River was the place to improve, not, as Stephen A. Douglas thought, that of the Calumet.

Which of these observers were mad? None of them, for everything that they said is true. Chicago is all things to all men, "queen and guttersnipe of cities," as George Warrington Stevens called her, "cynosure and cesspool of the world!" None of her lovers have ever championed her as a blameless girl who has always kept her pinafore clean; they have simply said that she has a vitality about her which makes others stale. Her very name is ambiguous. In the Indian languages it has been held to mean onion, garlic, and even skunk, but Milo M. Quaife has now shown pretty clearly that its essential reference was to anything strong or great. Chicago has barbarously destroyed her own past—even the Auditorium escaped destruction by a hair—yet she almost got the Old State House away from Boston when it seemed to be falling into neglect, and she once made a bid for Shakespeare's birthplace! The English reformer W. T. Stead blasted her in *If Christ Came to Chicago*, yet he ended the book with a utopian vision: "Whether or not Chicago will ever become the ideal city of the world is for the future to say; certainly she more than any other city, has the opportunity at her feet." And though Fredrika Bremer did not like the physical aspect of the place, she found the people "agreeable," "delightful," "good," "handsome," and "intellectual," a view strongly seconded by Harriet Martineau: "It is a remarkable thing to meet such an assemblage of educated, refined and wealthy persons as may be found there, living in small inconvenient houses on the edge of the wild prairie."

But did God or man make Chicago? Joseph Kirkland made a character in *The McVeys* (1888) declare that "when Providence shoved a line of great lakes away up into the heart of the grandest farm He ever laid out, and then put a harbor up at the furthest point in the line, He didn't leave much for men to do!" This would seem as much of an overstatement as Robert Herrick's contradictory remark in *The Gospel of Freedom* (1898), that "Chicago is an instance of a successful, contemptuous disregard of nature by man." Of course Chicago was strategically located. In the days of waterways and in the days of railroads, she was a natural focusing-point for the lumber of the North, the manufactured goods of the East, and the crops from the West; and now that the St. Lawrence waterway has been completed, she has become a world port besides. Moreover, though Chicagoans love to abuse their climate, it is still a healthy and invigorating one; the lake serves as a moderating influence, as well as a never-failing source of beauty and refreshment, and the rapid changes in temperature, sometimes as great as thirty degrees within a few hours, help to keep life from growing stagnant. But vigor was stimulated even more by the heroic tasks which, contrary to Joseph Kirkland, God left for man to do. The river was not deep enough for large boats nor the land dry enough for heavy wagons, portions of the downtown district have been raised ten feet or more to prevent the city from sinking into the mud, and the most beautiful parts of the lake shore have been built by man out of debris from the city itself. The river, "a sluggish, slimy stream, too lazy to clean itself," crowded the business district into a small, uncomfortable area and continually interrupted the flow of traffic at its many bridges; and as the city grew, it became a foul-smelling cesspool carrying contamination to the drinking water of the lake and remained such for many years until an engineering miracle reversed its flow.

II

Chicago's great opportunity to display herself as a center of civilization came with the World's Columbian Exposition, held (one year late) in 1893. She was an old hand at fairs. There had been a big agricultural fair on the lake front as early as 1859, and during the Civil War the Northwestern Sanitary Fair had been a roaring success. In 1873 a great cupolaed Interstate Industrial Exposition building had been erected on Michigan Avenue, where it stayed until it was torn down in 1891 to make room for the Art Institute. But none of this prepared the nation or the world or Chicago herself for what was very likely the most beautiful thing ever created in the Western Hemisphere. Saint-Gaudens called the association of artists it involved the greatest since the fifteenth century, and the Fine Arts Building (now rebuilt in stone as the Museum of Science and Industry) the most beautiful edifice since the Par-

thenon, but the total impact of the scene, in its accumulated splendor and activity, can scarcely be imagined.

The dedication exercises were held on May 1, 1893, a
chill and misty spring morning. When President Cleveland
arrived, with Governor Altgeld and the fair dignitaries,
they drove through the Midway, where, we are told, the
demonstration of variegated foreign cries which greeted
them "for penetrating power exceeded anything ever
heard in a political meeting." Besides the speeches by the
officers of the fair and political celebrities, there were ad-
dresses by Chauncey M. Depew and Henry Watterson
and a prayer by Cardinal Gibbons, but few among the
150,000 present were able to hear anything except the
singing by a chorus of 5,000 voices. Women and children
were held aloft in the crowd to save them from injury, and
seventeen persons fainted.

At the close of his address, Cleveland pressed a button
which started the power plant.

"The Stars and Stripes fluttered up the mast in the center
of the plaza, the red flag of Castille up another mast, and
the white initialed banner of Ferdinand and Isabella up another. On all sides, on the tall domes and cornices of the
buildings, flags furled for hours now broke out. From the
MacMonnies fountain and its companions the white water
gushed. The shroud fell from the Liberty statue, and it
glittered in the sun. . . .

"With all this rose the rumble of machinery set off by
the electric spark; from the lake came the booming of
guns from warships, starting flights of gulls from their
beach coverts."

To attempt to describe the Exposition adequately would
require a much larger book than this one. It lives in pictorial record and in the numerous fictions it inspired—

books like Clara Louise Burnham's *Sweet Clover* (1894) and Frances Hodgson Burnett's *Two Little Pilgrims' Progress* (1895), of which it forms the essential subject, and many others, like Robert Herrick's *Waste* (1924), in which it supplies an episode. For the moment, let us satisfy ourselves with what Hubert H. Bancroft saw, as recorded in *The Book of the Fair:*

"Let us imagine ourselves standing at eventide in the central court . . . haunted by the shadows of deserted temples east athwart the plaza. Toward the east darkness is setting on the waters of the lake. Northward and to the west a heavy pall of smoke broods over the great midcontinent metropolis, and far to the south the lurid flames of a blast furnace are faintly visible on the dusky horizon. Suddenly a beam of light shoots like a falling star from the lofty dome of the Administration building, and a moment later its symmetrical outlines stand out in tracery of fire. At its base is a circling wheel of light, and a hundred torches further relieve the black abyss beyond. Meanwhile a thousand lamps, clustered around the central avenue, have turned the night into day. Thus also the other great buildings that encircle the court assume their robes of light, with pillars, porticos, and colonnades blending in weird, yet brilliant perspective, like the threshold of an enchanted palace.

"From the summit of the Manufactures building a pyramid of dazzling light is cast on the dome of the Administration building, throwing into strong relief its delicate tracery of gold and white. Then in swiftly changing streams of white, green, and blue, purple, yellow, and scarlet, three search-lights are turned simultaneously on the central court, the basin, the MacMonnies fountain, and the statuary here displayed in lavish profusion. In the heroic statue of the republic, with its background of double columns shining like pillars of Carrara marble, every inch of its golden surface glitters beneath the piercing rays. Presently the search-lights sweep the horizon, one of them resting for a moment on the graceful figure of Diana poised against the sky as though suspended in midair. Another is turned toward the lake, casting its bright sheen on the waters of Michigan, and striking the sails of a passing vessel, whose white wings slowly vanish from sight. Gradually the scene grows warmer in its wealth of coloring, and the lights and shades more intense in contrast, the copses and groves of wooded island, with its garb of verdure, throwing their shadows across the tracery of fire.

"But the climax of all the brilliant display is in the electric fountains of the head of the lagoon in front of the Administration building. Here are light effects of surpassing loveliness, in rich varying hues, sprays, jets, and columns of water appearing as though ablaze in the glow of these powerful electric currents. Between them is the Mac-Monnies fountain, its waters iridescent as the rainbow, the centerpiece with its group of figures resembling a phantom ship with phantom crew, beautiful but with an unearthly beauty. Under these changing colors the vessel seems to float, now on a sea of white, and again on a rose-colored expanse, in frosted silver or on molten gold. Near by gondolas and electric launches speed swiftly to and fro across the lagoon, breaking its resplendent surface into a thousand glittering fragments, while from the plaza strains of music are wafted into the still night air, and above all is heard the ceaseless murmur of the waves, breaking on the shore adjacent, as with the low monotone of the ocean."

The idea of a great exposition to commemorate the discovery of America goes back at least as far as a series of letters from Spain by Clarence W. Bowen in *The Inde-*

pendent in 1884. The East regarded Chicago's bid as ridiculous; "Porkopolis" was not a civilized place; indeed the social arbiter Ward McAllister was uncertain about the whole idea, since, "in a social way, Columbus was an ordinary man." After the city had been chosen, the selection of the particular site still gave difficulty. At one time the lake front south of Monroe Street was favored; Carter Harrison, who lived on the West Side, wanted Garfield Park. The Jackson Park area on the South Side that was finally selected was largely unimproved—"three ridges of sandbars parallel with the shore; the intervening swales covered by boggy vegetation." The soil was water-soaked and subject to flooding. In twenty months, said Charles H. Burnham, seven hundred acres had to be "converted into a site suitable for an exposition of the industries and the entertainment of representatives of all the nations of the world. On its stately terraces a dozen palaces were to be built—all of great extent and of high architectural importance—these to be supported by two hundred other structures. Great canals, basins, lagoons and islands were to be constructed. The standard of the entire work was to be up to a degree of excellence which should place it on a level with the monuments of other ages."

The landscaping was in the hands of Frederick Law Olmsted; in the general scheme of the buildings, Burnham seems to have been the greatest force, especially after the death of his partner, John W. Root. Many great architects, East and West, were employed, but more than sixty structures, including the Fine Arts Building, were entrusted to Charles B. Atwood.

Both preparatory winters (1891–92 and 1892–93) were horrible on the lake front. Seven hundred of the seven thousand workmen employed were injured, and eighteen were killed. On January 10, 1891, Burnham took the architects out to the site. "It was a cold winter day; the sky was overcast with clouds and the Lake was covered with foam. ... Robert Peabody climbed up on a pier and called down: 'Do you mean to say that you really propose opening a Fair here by '93?' 'Yes,' I replied, 'we intend to.' 'It can't be done,' he said. 'That point is settled,' I replied."

The main buildings required twenty thousand tons of iron and steel, seventy million feet of lumber, and thirty thousand tons of "staff," which was a stucco-like combination of plaster of Paris and jute or other fiber. The Woman's Building, designed by Sophia G. Hayden, and exhibiting women's work from primitive times to modern artistic, medical, and eleemosynary activities was the first completed. This was the first great fair in which women had been importantly represented, and the able, indefatigable queen of Chicago society, Mrs. Potter Palmer, was chairman of the Board of Lady Managers. But the largest building—indeed the largest in the world—was the Manufactures and Liberal Arts Building, which could seat three hundred thousand people and was described, in typical booster "Windy City" fashion, as four times the size of the Roman Colosseum. Over the central dome of the Agricultural Building, designed by McKim, Mead and White, towered Saint- Gaudens's Diana, transferred from White's Madison Square Garden, where prudish New Yorkers had found her nudity disturbing. "What nonsense!" exclaimed Mrs. Palmer, when the question of propriety was raised in Chicago. "We will have it on the Woman's Building." Indeed there was enough nakedness closer to the eye so that nobody ought to have been disturbed by Diana, though some draperies were still absurdly discreet.

Electricity Hall aimed "to display with competitive

tests the working of electrical apparatus in practical use" and also "to present a history of this science from its very inception, with models, and in some instances the actual appliances used by the earlier inventors." The Transportation Building exhibited "every method of transportation, except the back of the mule and the foot of man." The railroads got the lion's share as "most important," but bicycles received "the attention to which their popularity and rapidly increasing use entitle them." The Government Building exhibits drew upon the Executive department, the Smithsonian Institution, the Fisheries Commission, and the National Museum for articles and materials to "illustrate the function and administrative facility of the government in time of peace, and its resources as a war power."

Henry Adams saw the dynamo in Chicago and lived to shudder over it as a symbol of the modern "multiverse," replacing the medieval universe which had centered in the Blessed Virgin. Krupp, simultaneously, was exhibiting the biggest gun in the world, with a range of sixteen miles. Electric power and elevated railroads were demonstrated; the Fair itself had the first third rail in the world. Women saw previews of many of the gadgets which have since delivered them from household slavery (and turned their husbands over, bound hand and foot, to the service men), including a "miniature ammonic ice-plant, which will be arranged to cool the entire house on hot days and nights." Steinert exhibited Bach's clavichord, Mozart's spinet, Haydn's and Beethoven's pianos. Elsewhere might be seen Columbus' contract with Ferdinand and Isabella, the Liberty Bell, Queen Victoria's needlework, Peregrine White's cradle, John Alden's Bible, Myles Standish's pipe, and an infinite variety besides.

The German government erected a sixteenth-century
Renaissance house which long outlived the Fair (it burned
in 1925, as did the Japanese House on Wooded Island), and
the reproduction of the Columbus caravels from Spain
(the Chicago producer Selig later made a three-reel film
around them, *The Coming of Columbus*). The French
erected a classical pavilion, and the English put up Victoria
House of terra cotta and oak timbers. The Massachusetts
state building reproduced John Hancock's house on Beacon Street, Pennsylvania modeled itself on Independence
Hall, New Jersey on Washington's headquarters at Mor-
ristown, and Virginia on Mount Vernon, while Florida
turned to old Fort Marion and California to the Spanish
missions.

The Exposition might have had a good many exhibits
which were turned down. One man wanted to build a
tower three thousand feet high, another a four-hundred-
story building, still another a suite of apartments under the
waters of Lake Michigan. Bull fights and cock fights were
offered, and the never-failing exponents of perpetual motion and squaring the circle wished to be on hand. The
Messiah offered himself also, and one person wished to
show a hag half made up into a beauty and transform the
other half of her before the eyes of the audience.

Some of these lunatics might have been quite at home
on the Midway, which stretched the whole distance from
Jackson to Washington parks. To Miss Berry of *Sweet
Clover* the Midway was "just a representation of matter"
as the White City was "an emblem of mind." The Midway
was "some dirty and all barbaric," its worst inhabitants
"avaricious and bad" and the best "just children in their
ignorance," and she thought that perhaps dying might be
"somethin' like crossin' the dividin' line that separates the

Midway from the White City." But aside from the fact that alcoholic drinks were sold in dry territory, there does not seem to have been much that was really wicked about the Midway. Many speak and write as if it consisted wholly of the Ferris Wheel and "Little Egypt," just as many 1933–34 writers were to describe the Century of Progress Exposition wholly in terms of the Skyride and Sally Rand. Yet in contemporary records of the World's Columbian Exposition, "Little Egypt" is hardly mentioned, nor is her name in the index of Bancroft's whole immense *Book of the Fair!*

Bancroft did describe the Midway, however, and we may as well again take him as our guide: "Entering the avenue a little to the west of the Woman's building they [visitors to the fair] would pass between the walls of mediaeval villages, between mosques and pagodas, past the dwellings of colonial days, past the cabins of South Seas islanders, of Javanese, Egyptians, Bedouins, Indians, among them huts of bark and straw that tell of yet ruder environment. They would be met on their way by German and Hungarian bands, by the discord of Chinese cymbals and Dahometan tom-toms; they would encounter jugglers and magicians, camel-drivers and donkey-boys, dancing girls from Cairo and Algiers, from Samoa and Brazil, with men and women of all nationalities, some lounging in oriental indifference, some shrieking in unison or striving to outshriek each other, in the hope of transferring his superfluous change from the pocket of the unwary pilgrim. Then, as taste and length of purse determined, for fees were demanded from those who would penetrate the hidden mysteries of the plaisance, they might enter the Congress of beauty with its plump and piquant damsels, might pass an hour in one of the theaters or villages, or partake of harmless beverages served by native waiters. Finally they would betake themselves to the Ferris Wheel, on which they were conveyed with smooth, gliding motion to a height of 260 feet, affording a transient and kaleidoscopic view of the park and all that it contains."

The Ferris Wheel seemed wicked only to those who saw it as tempting Providence. Robert Lawson's last book, *The Big Wheel*, weaves an entertaining story around its development by the Pittsburgh engineer, G. W. G. Ferris, as an engineering marvel to match the Eiffel Tower, which was constructed for the Paris exposition of 1889. It comprised two wheels, each 320 feet in circumference, set thirty feet apart, and carrying thirty-six luxurious cars, each twenty-seven feet long and capable of accommodating forty passengers. It gave a twenty-minute ride and at night was illuminated by 2,500 electric lights.

The Midway had German, Austrian, Moroccan, South Seas, and Irish villages. There was every variety of exotic theater, every variety of exotic food, every variety of music and noise. There were a Roman house, a Moorish palace, a Persian harem, and a Japanese bazaar. Tall Russians from Siberia jostled dwarfs from Africa. Eskimos sweltered in their furs through the Chicago summer until a baby, born at the fair, died, and the authorities ordered lighter clothing. Bohemian glass was blown and Vienna pastry baked. The Hagenbeck Zoo exhibited, and James J. Corbett demonstrated the punch that had vanquished John L. Sullivan. There were panoramas of the volcano of Kilauea and of the Alps at Berne. There was even a model of St. Peter's, one-sixtieth the size of the original. No, the Midway was by no means all frivolity.

But there can be no question that those who desired frivolity—and worse—in Chicago that summer were able to find it. This was one summer the downtown theaters did not have to shut down, especially not the Columbia, where Chicago's own Lillian Russell was holding forth. Buffalo Bill's Wild West show was in the old Coliseum on Sixty-third Street, where William Jennings Bryan would soon talk about the Cross of Gold. At Battery D (Michigan and Monroe), Florenz Ziegfeld of the Chicago Musical College established the Trocadero, but the music he provided proved too civilized for the fair crowds; he turned it over, accordingly, to his son, the future entrepreneur of the *Follies*, who put on less austere entertainments.

Theatrically speaking, however, the Exposition could easily have been more impressive. There was a Zoöpraxi-scopic Hall, "in which are given illustrated lectures on ani-mal locomotion as applied to art," and Eadweard Muy-bridge, who had conducted the race-horse experiment for Governor Leland Stanford in the seventies and thus earned his niche in motion picture history, was there, but Steele MacKaye, the greatest master of stagecraft that this coun-try ever produced, and his Spectatorium should have been and were not. As A. Nicholas Vardac has fascinatingly de-scribed it in his *Stage to Screen* (Harvard University Press, 1949), MacKaye developed a kind of "pictures-in-the-round-in-motion," or "three-dimensional motion pictures" which were to constitute "no pictorial illusion of reality but reality itself." The theme, inevitably, was Columbus, and the frame of the stage picture was to measure 150 by 70 feet, with the spectator's full range of vision extending more than 400 feet. "The entire stage apparatus was to be powered by electricity and the performance controlled from beginning to end by one man from a centrally located overhead booth. The building was in the process of construction . . . when the financial 'panic of '93' occurred. After hundreds of thousands of dollars had been invested and the building already in its final stages, for want of a few thousand dollars more the entire project was scrapped and, soon after, the building torn down, not one public performance having been given."

If the Midway served as the entertainment annex to the Exposition, there was another much more serious "World's Congress Auxiliary," meeting in the newly completed Art Institute, which aimed to supplement the display of material progress in the fair itself by portraying the "wonderful achievements of the new age in science, literature, education, government, jurisprudence, morals, charity, religion and other departments of human activity, as the most effective means of increasing the fraternity, progress, prosperity and peace of mankind." The Parliament of Religions was the portion which attracted most attention, for here, under secular auspices, was a kind of forerunner of the ecumenical conferences of today. It is interesting that though the Archbishop of Canterbury refused to cooperate on the ground that such a conference tacitly classified Christianity as merely one among many religions, both Cardinal Gibbons and the Roman Catholic archbishop of Chicago participated, and if the Orientals "stole the show" with their brilliant robes, there is also evidence that their spiritual idealism and serenity of spirit impressed many. From 1893 on, it began to be harder to talk about "the heathen." With what was called "Comparative Religion" there came a vision of an infinitely varied praying world, raising many-colored hands toward a universal God in the spirit of Christ's neglected words, "Other sheep have I that are not of this fold."

III

It is sometimes forgotten that the World's Columbian Exposition was held in a panic year and that the winter which followed, in Chicago and elsewhere, was one of bitter and cruel want, so that in many ears the new song, "After the Ball," which was played all summer, must have taken on a sinister note in retrospect. The fair started so quietly that at first it seemed bound to fail, but the official figures finally showed 27,539,531 admissions. The peak attendance—700,000—was on Chicago Day, the anniversary of the Fire, October 9, though it is said that many loyal Chicagoans went through the turnstiles again and again to boost the attendance figure as high as possible. In distant towns and villages, people spent their savings and put mortgages on their homes, and one countryman was overheard telling his wife, "Well, Susan, it paid, even if it did take all the burial money."

For what? For a dream of "progress" ending in a blind alley? Yes, but for something else too. For beauty. "Never before," wrote W. T. Stead, "have I realized the effect which could be produced by architecture." "It is the greatest thing that ever came into my life," declared the unromantic William Dean Howells. "It gives verity and value to everything. . . . There never was and there may never be again anything so beautiful."

"All at once," wrote Theodore Dreiser, "and out of nothing in this dingy city . . . which but a few years before had been a wilderness of wet grass and mud flats . . . had now been reared this vast and harmonious collection of perfectly constructed and showy buildings, containing, in their delightful interiors, the artistic, mechanical and scientific achievements." That was the essence of the White City. It would have been wonderful anywhere. In Chicago it was a miracle. Even Robert Herrick's narrator in *The Memoirs of an American Citizen,* haunted by "the skeleton that lay at the feast, the dread of want and failure that was stealing over all business," was willing to be "happy and without fear" in the lovely night: "The long lines of white buildings were ablaze with countless lights. . . . In that lovely hour, soft and gentle as was ever a summer's night, the toil and trouble of men, the fear that was gripping men's hearts in the market, fell away from me, and in its place came Faith. The people who could dream this vision and make it real . . . their sturdy wills and strong hearts would rise above failure, would press on to greater victories than this triumph of beauty. . . ."

This was the line generally taken by sensitive persons at the fair who were not mere aesthetes. Wrote Ernest Poole: "It was America saying:

" 'Look. Someday we shall come to this. Someday we'll have finished with all our grime and disorder and haste. Someday we'll have time for a world of beauty and leisure —far ahead.' "

The Chicago Plan, fathered by Burnham himself, was the legitimate child of the World's Columbian Exposition, and though the plan is still far from complete realization, what has been done is impressive enough to make any city proud. Of course, the Black City is still there. Of course, vice and crime are still there. But the dream must come first. The Sermon on the Mount did not inaugurate the millennium.

Like everything that is human, the fair had its failures. In July, seventeen firemen burned to death before 130,000 spectators in a warehouse fire. On October 28, at the very end, Carter Harrison was murdered by a crazy office seeker in the doorway of his hospitable Ashland Avenue home. More of the buildings should have been saved, and if a choice had to be made of the sculpture, it would have been better to keep the MacMonnies fountain than "Big Mary," the statue of the Republic which was surely not one of Daniel French's great works. More buildings might have been saved if it had not been for the fire of July 5, 1894, which burned the glorious Peristyle, opening out on the lake, Richard Hunt's beautiful Administration Building, and a number more. "Chicago," said Stead, "great in executing enterprises which can be executed under the stress and strain of a strong stimulus, is not equally great in preserving and maintaining that which she has created."

In retrospect the endless and indecisive controversy over Sunday opening seems asinine. The exhibition of painting and sculpture might have been more impressive if the federal government had had the wit to lift the tariff from works of art. And certainly there can be no excuse for the martyrdom Theodore Thomas was called upon to undergo. When the Steinway company foolishly decided not to exhibit at the Exposition, it was decided to use no Steinway pianos at the concerts. Paderewski refused to play on any other instrument, and Thomas smuggled a Steinway into the hall for him. Therefore the *Herald* and *Post* attacked both Paderewski (who had insulted this country by playing the work of low foreigners like Chopin and Schumann, instead of good American music) and Thomas, demanding the latter's removal. What is more amazing, *Musical Courier* joined in the attack on the megalomaniac, "not a native American," who pursued a "dictatorial and foolish policy of self-aggrandisement" under the impression "that the World's Fair was especially gotten up for his individual glory." The National Board heeded the outcry and ordered Thomas removed; but since his contract was with the Board of Directors, who stood by him, he continued playing until in August a cry arose to cut expenses, when he resigned. To its lasting honor, the *Tribune* denounced "this attempt to humiliate and persecute the man that has done more than any other for the cause of music in the United States. . . . It is too late in that long and honorable career for even members of the National Commission from the great art centers of Wyoming, Virginia, Utah, Kansas, and Arkansas to injure his fame."

The most serious charge made against the Exposition, by all means, was that of Louis Sullivan, who argued that it had delayed the development of American architecture by fifty years. I yield to no one in my admiration for Sullivan as an architect; as an architectural dogmatist he could be somewhat less endearing. If he had lived to see the abortions of the Century of Progress Exposition, where sanity was preserved only in such erections as Fort Dearborn, the Lincoln cabin, and the Colonial Village, or if he could see such a madman's nightmare as the Marina Apartments today, or the acres of glass boxes which are turning every city in the civilized world into a horror, he might perhaps have learned how valiantly the Exposition functioned to hold off the flood of architectural inhumanity which now engulfs us.

As a matter of fact, the architecture of the World's Columbian Exposition was not, as Sullivan would suggest, exclusively classical; many different styles were represented. I fear he might have been hurt by the remark made concerning his Transportation Building, with its golden entrance in terms of a series of receding circles, in a book by Glenn A. Bishop and Paul T. Gilbert called *Chicago's Accomplishments and Leaders* (1932)—"a striking example of the Chicago school of architecture established by Louis Sullivan. It is somewhat reminiscent of the Moorish."

Chicago was loath to give up talking about the White City. When I was a child, there was an amusement park so named on Sixty-third Street, whose central feature was a tall tower, magnificently illuminated by colored lights. Even after the rides were gone, the dance hall survived, and along with it the tower, until at last it burned, like the fair buildings themselves. But there is a much more important survival in the "Alma Mater" song, still sung by students of the University of Chicago, which, interestingly enough, was just getting started in Exposition days, and if you could not see it from the Midway, you could from the Ferris Wheel. The words were written by Edwin H. Lewis, then on the university staff, later dean of Lewis Institute, father of Janet Lewis, the novelist, and himself the author of *Those About Trench*. It was first sung by the Men's Glee Club at Central Music Hall, March 8, 1894.

> To-day we gladly sing the praise
>   Of her who owns us as her sons;
> Our loyal voices let us raise,
>   And bless her with our benisons.
> Of all fair mothers, fairest she,
>   Most wise of all that wisest be,
> Most true of all the true, say we,
>   Is our dear Alma Mater.
>
> Her mighty learning we would tell,
>   Tho' life is something more than lore;
> She could not love her sons so well,
>   Loved she not truth and honor more.
> We praise her breadth of charity,

Her faith that truth shall make men free,
That right shall live eternally,
We praise our Alma Mater.

The City White hath fled the earth,
But where the azure waters lie,
A nobler city hath its birth,
The City Gray that ne'er shall die.
For decades and for centuries,
Its battlemented towers shall rise,
Beneath the hope-filled western skies,
'Tis our dear Alma Mater.

2

"I Will!"

As Harry Hansen has pointed out in his lovely book on the Chicago River, early Chicago history has been conveniently summarized by the four pylons on the Michigan Avenue Bridge which now spans the distance between old Fort Dearborn and the Wrigley Building and Tribune Tower. "The east pylon at the north end of the bridge celebrates the Discoverers—Joliet, Marquette, La Salle and Tonty, who 'typify the spirit of brave adventure' in the white man's development of the Middle West. The west pylon commemorates the Pioneers and specifically mentions John Kinzie, fur trader, who settled near this spot and was 'one of a band of courageous pioneers who, with their lives at stake, struggled through the wilderness, breaking soil for the seeds of a future civilization.' The west pylon at the south end of the bridge is called Defense and commemorates the Fort Dearborn massacre of 1812. Those who fell 'will be cherished as martyrs in our early history.' On the east pylon stands Regeneration, commemorating the great fire of October, 1871, which devastated the city, whereupon the citizens rebuilt a new and greater city, 'imbued with the indomitable spirit and energy by which they have ever been guided.' "

The French discoverers, then, are the first names in Chicago history, but, as Milo M. Quaife says, "it seems probable that Chicago was an important meeting-place for Indian travellers long before the first white man came," and "who the first white visitor . . . was cannot be stated with certainty." Jean Baptiste Point Sable, who, in Quaife's view, has too often been regarded "with feelings mingled of levity and contempt," is generally called Chicago's first citizen. His mother was probably a Negro slave; his father seems to have belonged to "the ancient and widespread family of Dandonneau *dit* Du Sable, one of the most notable in the annals of Canada and of the Northwest." Even if we do not admire Point Sable, however, we can surely admire Mrs. La Compt, who died at Cahokia in 1843 at the age of 109. She had great influence with the Potawatomis, and when an Indian attack was contemplated, they would warn her in the night. "Instead of seeking her own safety, however, she would set out alone to meet the hostile war party, and never failed to avert the storm and prevent bloodshed. She sometimes remained with the warriors for days, appeasing their anger and urging wise counsels upon them. In due time the anxious villagers, who had been watching meanwhile with arms in their hands for the expected attack, would see Mrs. La Compt approach at the head of a band of warriors, their angry passions stilled and their war paint changed to somber black to manifest their sorrow for having entertained hostile designs against their friends."

Beginning as a village, Chicago received a city charter in 1837, which soon proved an inadequate instrument to enable her to meet the problems arising from her growing population. There was a new constitution in 1870; but the constant tug of war between the city and the state of Illinois, which has always feared domination by the young giant at the foot of Lake Michigan, has never come to an end.

Until not very long ago the City of Chicago, Cook County, the Board of Education, the Public Library Board, the Sanitary District, the Lincoln Park Board, the West Park Board, and the South Park Board each had independent taxing powers, and each operated under its own rules. Some of these governing bodies were elected, others appointed; moreover, while the Lincoln Park and West Park boards were appointed by the governor of Illinois, the South Park board was appointed by the judges of the circuit court of Cook County!

There have been times when the "I Will" spirit has faltered; there are still those who think that Chicago might have had the automobile industry instead of Detroit if the city had been awake to her opportunity. There were those who opposed the Illinois and Michigan Canal when it opened in 1848 and gave Chicago access to the Gulf of Mexico because they feared it would benefit St. Louis, not Chicago. And when the city's first mayor, William B. Ogden, set out to promote the Chicago and Galena Railroad, Chicago merchants opposed him, arguing that if farmers could ship their products in instead of bringing them, it would destroy Chicago as a market center; but the indomitable Ogden went out and sold his stock to the farmers themselves, and the "I Will" spirit was on top again. It manifested itself somewhat differently when the Prince of Wales (later Edward VII) visited Chicago and was introduced by Mayor "Long John" Wentworth with, "Boys, this is the Prince of Wales," and when the royal visitor thoughtlessly spat into a ship while it was being loaded at the Rush Street Bridge, Wentworth cried out: "Stop that,

young man! Don't you know any better than to spit into
a load of grain?"

In pre–Civil War Chicago, the abolitionists and their
supporters were pitted against Stephen A. Douglas, who
was in and out of popular favor, depending upon how the
tides of opinion flowed. In 1850 the Chicago Common
Council classified supporters of the Fugitive Slave Law
with Judas and Benedict Arnold. Chicago was an important station on the underground railroad, and Frémont carried it in 1856, though Buchanan carried Illinois.

Medill and the *Tribune* were important in securing the
nomination of Lincoln at the Wigwam on Lake Street in
1860, but he paid little attention to their wishes in making
appointments. In 1861 the *Tribune*, which expected a short
war, thought Illinois capable of raising all the ninety-four
regiments then required, but early in 1865, Medill participated in a protest visit to Washington, demanding that
Chicago's quota be lowered, only to be sternly rebuked by
Lincoln, who declared that Chicago, and the *Tribune* in
particular, had been the chief instrument after Boston in
bringing on the war. The *Tribune* called for the draft,
emancipation, and the use of Negro troops long before
they came. Not always satisfied with Lincoln's policies, she
was nevertheless a strong war paper, and it has been said
that she was the only big paper to run the Gettysburg Address on the front page.

The war brought tremendous prosperity to Chicago—
Stanton said that without McCormick's reaper the North
could not have won—and partly in consequence, war fever
in the city ran high. The Irish, Democrats almost to a
man, were suspected of Southern sympathies, but many
enlisted and became war heroes. Allan Pinkerton, of secret
service fame, was a Chicagoan; so were George F. Root

("The Battle Cry of Freedom"; "Tramp, Tramp, Tramp"; etc.) and Henry C. Work ("Marching Through Georgia"), whose war songs contributed much to morale. To the tremendously successful Sanitary Commission Fair of 1863, Lincoln donated a perfected draft of the Emancipation Proclamation, which brought the highest price of any item —$3,000—thus winning the President a gold watch. When the news of Lincoln's assassination arrived in Chicago, young Melville Stone saw a man shot down in cold blood in the crowded rotunda of the Matteson House because he said the President deserved it. "There was no arrest. No one would have dared arrest the man. He walked out a hero."

But that too was wartime behavior, and it may be well to remember that in 1864 the city gave Lincoln less than a two-thousand-vote majority out of the total twenty-seven thousand votes cast. Illinois had a Copperhead legislature during the war, which elected an anti-war senator and was prorogued by Governor Yates to prevent its memorializing Congress to call a peace convention. The tension over the Copperhead *Times* in Chicago is described in another chapter. There was also much fear, some of it justified, of the rebel prisoners of war held at Camp Douglas, which was at Twenty-third Street and Cottage Grove Avenue.

II

When Chicago was incorporated in 1833, her population was 350. By 1850 she had nearly 30,000; by 1870, 300,000. In the eighties she passed Philadelphia as the second largest city. By 1900 her population was nearly 1,700,-000; by 1920, over 2,700,000. The 1950 census figure was 3,620,962, but by 1960 this had dropped to 3,550,404. As far back as the twenties the population of the suburbs was increasing more rapidly than that of the city proper, and it is entirely possible that Chicago may sometime have to yield the title of second city to Los Angeles. Chicago is still the greatest rail center and grain exchange in America, and Jules Verne's remark (*Around the World in Eighty Days*) that "trains are not wanting in Chicago" is still a prime understatement, but she must now share her packing supremacy with Kansas City and Omaha.

Her first settlers were largely native Americans, with New England predominating, but by 1845 there were already many foreign-born inhabitants. Until 1900 the bulk of the immigration was German, Irish, and Scandinavian; after that date came the influx from Eastern Europe. The first Jewish synagogue was established in 1847, but the early Jews were Germans, and they were not always gracious about welcoming their less aristocratic and sophisticated co-religionists from Russia and Poland, who arrived later and crowded into the ghettos around Maxwell Street and elsewhere. After World War I immigration from abroad was cut down, but Southern Negroes began moving up the Mississippi into Chicago, until there are now more than 800,000 of them.

Up to the Fire, Wabash and Michigan in what is now the downtown district were still residence streets. It may be that the glory of the West Side too was largely a pre-Fire affair, but the mayor of Chicago lived on Ashland Boulevard as late as the World's Columbian Exposition, and the marble fronts on Washington did not easily relinquish their pride. By 1890, Prairie Avenue, between South Sixteenth and Twenty-second, was "the" street, but it was already in decline by 1910, and by 1930 it was a slum. From there the fashionables turned to the near North Side, and the "Gold Coast" is still the best address in Chicago, though it has Lake Michigan licking its feet on one side and the beatnik slums infesting them on the other. For that matter, the North Side in general has probably held its character better than any other part of Chicago, though there are depressed areas here also, as there are many oases of charm or homeliness in other parts of the city. Like all large American cities, Chicago has found her civic problems accentuated by the fact that for many years the kind of people to whom she might reasonably have looked for leadership have been doing their business in the city but living in the suburbs. She has swallowed up Austin, Hyde Park, Lake View, Englewood, and many other communities, but both Evanston and Oak Park (the largest village in the world) have preserved their independence, and both, like the Shore towns north of Evanston, have remained "dry" despite the "wetness" of neighboring Chicago. There are also many attractive communities to the west of Oak Park, most of whose residents must, however, depend for commuting service upon railroads and interurban electrics instead of using the "L," as most Evanstonians and Oak Parkers do.

In early Chicago, as in most frontier communities, there was a tendency to blur social distinctions; servants sometimes attended the same parties as their masters, and when they were pretty enough they might even marry them. A certain amount of this simplicity always survived. The builders of Chicago never felt quite at home with ostentation, and they certainly did not consider idleness respectable simply because there was wealth in the family. Thus Marshall Field, who publicly expressed his contempt for genealogy, was not at all disturbed when he was told that a clerk was calling on his daughter. "Thank God," he said, "there is no disgrace in being a clerk." This same merchant prince allowed his coachman to drive him to the store, but when he arrived within a block of his destination, he got out and walked the rest of the way, arriving on foot, like other people.

Perhaps it was this respect for hard work which helped the Puritan standards of New England to survive as long as they did in Chicago society. Being sensitive men, both H. C. Chatfield-Taylor and Arthur Meeker were conscious of something sinister and tigerish in the life around them, but both have testified too that in general their friends were anything but "fast." This applies to both sex and drinking, though the latter was regarded somewhat more tolerantly on Ashland Boulevard, where Southern standards of hospitality tended to prevail. Mrs. Potter Palmer supported Frances Willard, and her successor as queen of Chicago society, Edith Rockefeller McCormick, who regarded herself as a reincarnation of the child-bride of Tutankhamen and surrounded herself with a protocol which passed the bounds of the fantastic, never served a drop of liquor in her home. In 1882 some of the clergy agitated the possibility of stopping Sunday papers, horse cars, and milk deliveries, and when the Auditorium was opened seven years later, there was solemn canvassing of the propriety of wearing décolleté gowns. As late as 1913 that most chaste and discreet of nudes, the "September Morn" of Paul Chabas, could not be exhibited in an art dealer's window without causing the proprietor to be haled into court, and Marshall Field's drew their window curtains on Sundays as late as World War I.

Yet when profits were involved, compromises could always be made. Thus the *Tribune* opposed prize fighting but ran prize-fight news, and the first full-page illustrated advertisement in the paper, April 12, 1878, was for liquor and cigars. When Jim Fisk was murdered over Josie Mansfield in 1872, the *Tribune* moralized over the "unholy love" —and printed their letters. Two years later they printed the love letters of Theodore Tilton and his wife, whom he had accused of criminal intimacy with her pastor, Henry Ward Beecher, placing them among the great love letters of the world.

Religious influences naturally reinforced some of the attitudes I have described, though the churches were far from being a unit on moral issues. As we have already seen, the name of a Catholic priest, Jacques Marquette, stands at the very beginning of Chicago's history, but the first parish priest was not assigned until 1833. The diocese of Chicago (now the largest archdiocese in America) was established in 1843; by 1890, the German influx had made the Lutherans the largest Protestant group, but the Catholics had seven and a half times as many people as the first seven Protestant groups together. It was the Methodists, however, who placed the first stationed minister in Chicago in 1831, and two years later Jeremiah Porter established the First Presbyterian Church, soon to be prominently identified with the antislavery cause in the city. The Baptists began the next year and the Episcopalians in 1834. By 1842–43 abolition had already split both the Baptists and the Presbyterians, and the First Congregational Church was organized in 1851 by ardent antislavery seceders from the Third Presbyterian. The temperance movement, too, was well under way by the forties, and though the Catholics, Lutherans, and other groups then largely of foreign extraction remained cold to it, it was aided notably after 1874 by the national leadership of Frances E. Willard of Evanston, through the Woman's Christian Temperance

Union, with its valuable educational work, demonstrating the ravages of alcohol. Sunday schools, sometimes as missions, date from 1843. By 1853 the Chicago City Missionary Society was needed to care for the "destitute and ignorant." The first notable revival was in 1837; by the fifties the Methodists had set up their summer camp grounds at Des Plaines. D. L. Moody arrived in Chicago from Boston in 1856, working first with delinquent boys, moving in and out of the city while he established his great reputation as an evangelist and lay interdenominational leader, and in 1889 founding, near Lincoln Park, the Moody Bible Institute, still a stronghold of midwestern evangelical fundamentalism. The YMCA reached Chicago in 1858, the YWCA in 1876, the Salvation Army in 1885. Most denominations established theological schools in the area, among them Garrett Biblical Institute (Methodist), Chicago Theological Seminary (Congregational), and the Presbyterian Theological Seminary of the Northwest, later known as McCormick.

Minority groups too found a haven in the city—the Swedenborgians in 1835 and both the Unitarians and the Universalists the year after. Spiritualists welcomed Mrs. Julia Lusk, a "rapping medium" from Milwaukee, in 1849. Christian Scientists incorporated in 1886 and dedicated their first church in 1897. The controversial Scot, John Alexander Dowie, founder of the "Christian Catholic Apostolic Church in Zion," was in the area by the nineties; in 1901 he founded his utopia, Zion City, in Lake County.

As early as the fifties, "Deacon" William Bross, scientist, lieutenant-governor, *Tribune* editor, and historian of Chicago, was trying to reconcile science and religion—there is still a lectureship which bears his name at Lake

Forest University—and long after he was gone, the *Tribune* could generally be counted upon to defend "heretics"; on May 21, 1881, they printed the entire new "Revised Version" of the New Testament in a Sunday issue (ninety-two compositors set it up in twelve hours); later they championed the historical-critical school of Bible study in the person of President Harper of the University of Chicago. The *Tribune* also championed—and printed the sermons of—David Swing, who resigned his Presbyterian pulpit in 1875, under accusation of heresy, and became the first pastor of Central Church, meeting first in McVicker's Theater, then in Central Music Hall, and, during Dr. Gunsaulus's ministry, in the Auditorium.

Among the movements for interdenominational co-operation and religious enlightenment in Chicago, I must not fail to mention the Sunday Evening Club, which has been meeting in Orchestra Hall ever since Clifford W. Barnes founded it in 1907. Designed "to maintain a service of Christian inspiration and fellowship in the business center of Chicago, and to provide for the moral and religious welfare of the city," it has widened the horizon of countless Chicagoans and given a hearing to virtually every outstanding religious leader. In 1922 it became one of the first religious services to go on the air. Fellowship between Christian and non-Christian groups had already been notably fostered by that enlightened, though often crotchety, good citizen, the German-born Emil G. Hirsch, rabbi of Sinai Temple from 1880 to 1912. Frankly proclaiming that he felt more fellowship with Unitarians and Ethical Culture people than with orthodox Jews, Hirsch held his services on Sunday morning and even took his texts from the New Testament when he liked, though treating them in an unorthodox fashion from the Christian point of view. Hirsch pulled no punches with Jew or Gentile, but in spite of his porcupine aspects, his ministry was one of reconciliation.

III

The first great enemy Chicago had to fight was mud, and there is more than humor in the oft-told stories of the street signs proclaiming "No bottom here" and "This way to China." Her first great job, accordingly was literally to pull herself up out of the mud, and George Pullman first came to fame when, in the fifties, he used five hundred men and twenty-five hundred jackscrews to lift the Tremont House eight feet "without disturbing a guest or cracking a cup." When streets were raised wooden sidewalks were often built on street level, high above the prairie, where they sheltered "millions of rats" and sometimes worse things; and because the builder did not always know just where the street would finally lie, he developed the "Chicago cottage," with a flight of outside steps leading to the main entrance on the second story. Necessarily the sidewalk did not always run on the same level even in a single block, and there is a very amusing passage about this in Clark E. Carr's novel, *The Illini* (1904): "As I was looking down Dearborn Street, I saw approaching us in the distance what appeared to be a giant. He walked a few steps upon a level with us on the sidewalk, then descended, his legs, his body, and finally his head disappearing, and then his head and body reappearing, but not his legs . . . and so he appeared and disappeared until finally he came up the steps to where we were. He was simply walking the streets toward us, up and down stairs, on a Chicago sidewalk as then constructed." This expanding and contracting giant was Chicago's famous mayor, "Long John" Wentworth.

Plank roads proved unsatisfactory because filth collected under the boards, but I saw the coming of asphalt streets and cement sidewalks in the neighborhood where I lived; until then many streets were paved with wooden blocks held together with tar or some similar substance. There had to be viaducts over railroad tracks where these ran on the ground, and because the river divided Chicago into three parts, there were bridges everywhere, forty-five of them by 1893, most of them swinging bridges, many operated by steam. Even today Michigan Avenue must lift itself high into the air, stopping all traffic in both directions, whenever even a private sailboat with masts too high to clear chooses to pass.

Horse railroad companies were chartered on the North and South sides in 1859. In 1860 there were ten separate corporations in the field; in 1870, twenty-six; in 1900, thirty-eight. Cable cars began in 1892 and disappeared in 1906, by which time the electrification begun in 1890 had been completed. The elevated roads were built between 1892 and 1900, the "Loop" being completed in 1897. The first "L" ran from Congress south to Thirty-ninth Street; this was extended to Jackson Park for the fair. The Lake Street line on the West Side came next. Steam engines were used at first, but after the use of electric power for transportation had been demonstrated at the fair, the roads canceled their orders for more engines and became the first electrically-operated commercial "L." Proposals to achieve unification and municipal ownership were defeated or nullified, for various reasons, at intervals between 1904 and 1930. In 1927 all the surface lines were placed under a single board, and by June 1958, all the street cars had been replaced by buses. In 1945 the Chicago Metropolitan Transit Authority unified the operation of all public transportation in the city.

Health problems were tackled with more determination and intelligence. In the early days sewage ran in the gutters and accumulated under wooden sidewalks; as late as the sixties, small fish sometimes passed through the water taps, and Bob Casey could remember that the newspapers of the nineties ran water reports alongside the weather reports, using a set of symbols to advise residents in various sections of the city whether it was safe to drink unboiled water. "The river stinks," cried the *Times* on one occasion. "The air stinks. People's clothing, permeated by the foul atmosphere, stinks. . . . No other word expresses it so well as stink. A stench means something finite. Stink reaches the infinite and becomes sublime in the magnitude of odiousness." The river had a right to stink, for it was the open sewer of the city, and though the Sanitary District began struggling with the problem in 1889, it was not solved, nor did Chicago learn how to stop polluting her water supply in Lake Michigan until 1900, when the flow of the river was reversed. Even this action needed to be supplemented by further engineering miracles, and even these did not produce a perfect solution (perhaps there are none in this world), so that there were complaints from Mississippi towns concerning the pollution of river waters and complaints from Canada that the level of Lake Michigan was being lowered. Nevertheless, deaths from typhoid fell from 1,489 in 1892 to 370 in 1905, to 30 in 1921, to 11 in 1928, and infant mortality from 4,238 in 1892 to 2,643 in 1905, to 1,669 in 1927.

Chicago's official seal contained the words "*Urbs in*

Horto" (a City in a Garden), which must seem ironical to those who today travel for blocks without seeing a tree or, in some sections, hardly a blade of grass. In the early days it was quite true, however. Margaret Fuller was charmed by the prairie flowers "which gemmed and gilt the grass" on the edge of the lake, and Fredrika Bremer exclaimed over sunflowers "four yards high" and asters higher than her head. William Corkran has left a very careful description of how the city looked when he arrived in 1868 to become librarian at the Historical Society: "In summer the North Side was by far the prettiest part of the city, with its numerous large gardens filled with the choicest flowers, its old trees grown to enormous size throwing their leafy shadows across street and sidewalk, presenting in many instances a perfect bower."

The Fire destroyed many Chicago trees; others could have been saved, just as a great many other things which are being destroyed today in Chicago and elsewhere could be saved if the human race had decency and a modicum of brains. At least it must be said of Chicago that though she destroyed her trees, she created a magnificent park and boulevard system, which since 1895 has been supplemented by an extensive system of beaches and since 1915 by fifty-one square miles of forest preserves, providing a wooded belt encircling the city everywhere except on her water side.

The first park in Chicago was Dearborn Park, which occupied the site where the Public Library now stands. Beginning in 1869 the city began creating the Gilbert-and-Sullivan-like chaos which she loves in civic affairs by setting up local park districts. Ultimately there were three large ones and nineteen small, each with its own commissioners and policies; not until 1935 were they unified into one Chicago Park District. Yet by 1893, Chicago had already spent $24,000,000 on eight large and twenty-nine small parks and squares, connected by thirty-five miles of boulevard.

The largest park in Chicago is Lincoln Park on the North Shore, and between the lake and the zoo, which began in 1874 with one lone bear cub—value ten dollars—nobody will ever convince any Chicago child that it is not also the best. It is true that, thanks to the generosity of Edith Rockefeller McCormick, who gave the land, and the unselfish devotion of people like John T. McCutcheon, who labored to bring it into being, the Lincoln Park Zoo now has a rival at Brookfield, southwest of the city, where animals are shown in barless cages; but this did not exist in the days of my youth, and even aside from its greater accessibility, the Lincoln Park establishment is still a great zoo by any standards. But for historically minded persons such as I, the park possessed an almost comparable attraction in its fine collection of monuments of great men, which helped me to develop some knowledge of biography but a much larger tendency toward hero-worship. There were no monuments in Douglas Park except one of the Bohemian patriot Havlíček, erected during my childhood, who meant nothing to me, though another West Side park, Garfield, had Robert Burns, who meant much, and one summer an impressive array of plaster casts of World's Columbian Exposition statuary was brought out—I have no idea where it had been or what became of it afterwards—and exhibited, a few pieces in Douglas Park but most of it in Garfield. I found it surpassingly beautiful, and since most of the figures were nude, I learned also that the human body is not shameful, despite all I had been taught to the contrary. In little Union Park, just off Ashland Boulevard, there was a statue of the elder

Carter Harrison and another monument which stimulated my imagination more; commemorating the Haymarket tragedy, it portrayed a policeman with his hand upraised: "In the name of the people of Illinois, I command peace."

Lincoln Park was originally Lake Park and was renamed after Lincoln's death. Before that, part of it had been a cemetery, and the tomb of Ira Couch, who built the Tremont House, is still there, as is the grave of David Kennison, survivor of the Fort Dearborn massacre, who died in 1852, aged 115 years. As we have seen elsewhere, the great South Side park, Jackson, developed largely in the wake of the World's Columbian Exposition; its neighbor, Washington Park, was the center for the sporting set until the race track was closed down. Besides Garfield and Douglas, the West Side has Humboldt Park, famous for its roses, and, newer and larger, and more primitively landscaped, Columbus Park, farther west. Lincoln and Garfield and Humboldt all have conservatories—Garfield's is particularly famous, and I shall never forget the sight and smell of the wonderful chrysanthemum shows I saw there—and so had Douglas when I was born. It faced Ogden Avenue, standing on ground now occupied by the formal gardens, and an 1893 handbook of Chicago declares that "decidedly the handsomest and costliest conservatory in any of the parks is the new $50,000 edifice recently erected . . . at Douglas Park." But some fool decided to pull it down while I was still very small, and today there must be very few people who know that it ever existed.

Grant Park, which stretches along the lake front of the downtown district, now, since Century of Progress days, supplemented by Burnham Park, farther out in the lake, is different from the other parks in that, although it contains its own wonders and beauties—of Buckingham Fountain it was not unreasonably said that Versailles had come to Chicago—the most wonderful thing about it is that it exists and gives Chicago such a valuable front yard and breathing space. Wonderful, too, is the fact that much of it was created of refuse—the refuse of the Fire, to begin with, and much later the earth dug out from under the streets of the Loop when the sixty-two-mile underground tunnel system was constructed there. What is not often enough remembered is that Chicago owes this great blessing to the devotion and public spirit of one man, A. Montgomery Ward, the mail-order merchant, for though buildings were barred in the area by an ordinance of 1837, everybody knows that city ordinances were made to be violated when it is to anybody's interest to do so, unless somebody else cares enough to fight for them. In this case, the city itself was the worst offender, for the city turned Grant Park into a dumping ground, and Montgomery Ward was the man who was enough concerned about it to spend his money on legal battles and endure unmerited abuse. There has also been much litigation involving the Illinois Central Railroad, which had been allowed to build its tracks along the lake front, here again partly because interests were involved but partly also because the railroad had undertaken to perform services that must otherwise have been performed by the city itself. The museums which have been erected in Grant Park since the final decision was handed down represent a kind of compromise with Ward's original idea, but most persons would probably call it a wise one. The only other erection is Soldier Field, dedicated Armistice Day, 1925, which has accommodated events as dissimilar as the Eucharistic Congress of 1926, the Tunney-

Dempsey prize fight of 1927, and the annual Chicagoland Music Festivals, none of which would seem to have had much to do with honoring dead soldiers.

IV

Whether manufacturing and merchandising constitute civilization or whether in our world they merely provide a basis upon which a metropolitan civilization may be built might be discussed at considerable length; in so limited a book as this one, some of these matters can be presented directly, while others, whatever the answer, can only exist implicationally. It is delightful that the most famous erection in the city which fathered the skyscraper should still be the quaint old pre-Fire Water Tower at Michigan and Chicago avenues. Though Oscar Wilde denounced it as "a castellated monstrosity with pepper boxes stuck all over it," it has become almost a symbol of the city itself.

The first attempt to solve the weight problem involved in erecting tall buildings was the raft of steel and concrete constituting a "floating foundation" which was first used by Burnham and Root in the Montauk Building of 1882. The last great buildings constructed of solid masonry on this principle were the sixteen-story Monadnock Block (Root and Burnham, 1889), whose walls are seven feet thick at the base, and the Auditorium Hotel and Theater (Dankmar Adler and Louis Sullivan, 1887–89), which has ten stories, with a seventeen-story tower weighing fifteen thousand tons, which had to be loaded artificially to provide for even settling. In 1883, trying to provide as much window space as possible, William LeBaron Jenney discovered the true skyscraper principle by using a skeleton-type of construction (wrought iron to the sixth story and Bessemer steel beams above) on the ten-story Home Insurance Building. Three years later, Holabird and Roche employed a complete, riveted steel frame from the foundation up in the Tacoma Building, and in 1891, Burnham and Root put up the twenty-two-story Masonic Temple, then the highest building in the world. With that the lid was off, to the vast satisfaction of everybody except the wise Mr. Dooley, who pointed out that the new buildings were not being called skyscrapers by the sky and that we had yet to produce sky-scraping men who did not need to be buried by hand.

But the Auditorium was not the first great Chicago hotel by any means. It was James Kinzie who built the first little inn at Wolf's Point in 1828. In 1831, Mark Beaubien opened the most famous pioneer hotel, the Sauganash Tavern; his violin playing nightly for dancing helped make it popular. The first brick hotel, with printed menus and napkins, was the Lake House, 1835. The first Tremont House was built in 1835, but it was the third, creation of Ira and James Couch, that was Chicago's first hotel of metropolitan proportions. About a year later came the Briggs House, Lincoln's headquarters during his campaign. Practically all first-class hotels burned in 1871, including the brand-new Palmer House and the Grand Pacific, yet within six years Chicago had sixteen first-class hotels, the Palmer House, the Grand Pacific, the Tremont, and the Sherman House being known as the "Big Four."

While the Tremont House was still burning, John B. Drake stopped in at the Michigan Avenue Hotel, on the site of the present Congress, and offered to buy it—$1,000 in cash and the rest in two weeks. Because they thought him mad, and the hotel sure to burn, they accepted the offer and drew up a contract. The hotel survived. Drake renamed it the Tremont House, enlarged it by taking in some adjoining buildings, and, having very little competition, did a rushing business. The second Palmer House opened in November, 1873. It had been designed in the French style by John Mills Van Osdel, and it cost $3,500,000. The Grand Pacific, owned and operated by John B. Drake, whom we have already met and whose sons were to build the Blackstone and the Drake, was famous among other things for its annual game dinner.

The restaurants of the nineties ranged from such fashionable places as Kinsley's, Rector's, and Henrici's (now surviving only in its reconstruction in the Museum of Science and Industry) to H. H. Kohlsaat's stool-and-counter restaurants, where a small meal cost a dime and a "superfluity" might be had for a quarter. John R. Thompson opened the first of his well-known cheap restaurants at Madison near La Salle in 1893. And no Chicagoan of my generation would dream of failing to mention Kranz's confectionery store on State Street near Washington, with its beautiful rounded glass windows and *objets d'art*, which survived into the 1940's. Modern hotels include, in the downtown district, the Sherman, Bismarck, La Salle, Morrison, and Stevens, now the Conrad Hilton, largest hotel in the world; on the North Side, the Ambassador, Sovereign, Belmont, Lake Shore Drive, Sheridan Plaza, Surf; on the South Side, the Chicago Beach, Cooper-Carlton, Shoreland, Flamingo, East End Park, and Southmoor.

In quality merchandising the great names are Marshall Field and Potter Palmer. In the early days they were together; in the sixties, when most stores had not even achieved uniform prices, Palmer's "on approval" and money-back guarantee policies were sensational. Later he was primarily a hotel man; more than any other he created both State Street (Lake Street was the first merchandising center) and the Gold Coast (when he built his Gothic castle on Lake Shore Drive in the mid-eighties, it was still a wilderness). Arthur Meeker found Palmer "common and flashy." There may be some justice in this; not even Dickens would have been able to think up a better stock name for a rich man. Kipling thought the silver dollars in the Palmer House barber shop floor Hottentotish, and though Palmer did not place them there, he may have admired them. He had his gay-blade aspects in his youth, and we are told that he once mused over his beautiful Kentucky-belle young wife at a reception and murmured, "There she stands with two hundred thousand dollars' worth of jewels on her." Nevertheless, he had vision and imagination and considerable social conscience. In the Panic of 1857 he told his customers that so long as he had a dollar, their credit was good at his store, and if he sometimes raised the rent on his tenants when their business was good, he voluntarily lowered it when business was bad, and if he believed in them, he would carry them when they could not pay at all. As for Mrs. Palmer, she was much more than a queen of society. Altgeld admired her; W. T. Stead nominated her for mayor of his Utopia-in-Chicago. She was interested in Hull-House, in factory legislation, and in women's welfare; she had superb taste as an art collector; she manifested her great executive capacity first as chairman of the Board of Lady Managers of the great fair, then, after her husband's death, in her masterly development of an agricultural empire in Florida. Mrs. Palmer might be exclusive about her party lists, but in exposition days she gave food, shelter, and transportation to anybody who needed it, and if somebody had to nurse a baby in her library, it did not trouble her at all.

Nobody ever accused Marshall Field of vulgarity; not even the $120,000,000 he left when he died in 1906 could

cheapen him. McCutcheon's cartoon showed Death closing a volume which ended with a reference to a man "about
whose fortune there has never been a suspicion of taint . . .
whose faith in Chicago has been steadfast and true, and
whose life will be a beacon light to guide future generations
to honorable success." It was all true. He was the perfect
merchant prince, as impressive exteriorly as Edwin Arling-
ton Robinson's Richard Cory, and without his internal
instability. Yet he had tragedy in his life. When his first
wife went to live in France, an old friend said to her husband, "Marshall, you have no home, no family, no happiness
—nothing but money," and Field did not reply. His Prairie
Avenue neighbors believed him to be in love with Delia
Caton long before her husband's death set her free to marry
him, and it is not melodramatic to say that it was his son's
death of a bullet wound that killed him. Chicago legendry
maintains that the son was murdered at the Everleigh Club,
but no evidence has ever been brought forth to substantiate
this, and Carter Harrison II, who was mayor at the time,
was convinced that there was nothing in it. Even then for
his father bitter grief kept company with perfect dignity.
"Aren't you ashamed?" Field asked the newspapermen who
swarmed about him upon his return to Chicago, and one
of them replied, "Yes, Mr. Field, I am." When he was gone,
a reporter asked Mrs. Field for his last words. "Mr. Field's
last words," replied the great lady, "were for me, not for
the world."

Field's great benefactions all came late in his life. He
might have been as great a philanthropist as Julius Rosenwald. It was not greed that held him back, for he was a man
of very modest wants, but lack of imagination. Cold though
he seemed to many, Field was a humane man. Drivers who
flogged their horses were through at Field's. "How many

boys came down without overcoats and mittens?" he asked
one cold morning. "Outfit them all and say nothing about
it." But even in his own business Field showed much less
inventiveness and capacity for experimentation than the
much flashier, though equally honorable, Harry Gordon
Selfridge, who was long his second-in-command and who
introduced so many valuable innovations, including window displays, personal services, and the establishment of a
bargain basement or "budget floor" that was to gross $25,-
000,000 yearly. It was with great reluctance that Field
finally agreed to allow Selfridge to open a tearoom: "This
is a dry-goods store; we don't feed people here!" Yet today
what Chicago woman could think of Field's without its
restaurant service? The very successful book department
began long after Field's death, under James Simpson, as did
the establishment of branch stores in Evanston, Oak Park,
and Lake Forest. Field did not even claim to work hard or
long hours. He disliked sending out traveling salesman from
the wholesale house because he considered it undignified.
He owed his success to his integrity, courtesy, gentility,
style, good taste, and devotion to quality.

Many other Chicago stores would be worth discussing
if space were available, especially Carson, Pirie, Scott and
Company, who still occupy the handsome building which
Louis Sullivan designed for Schlesinger and Meyer in 1900.
The Mandel Brothers were already in business in 1855,
and E. J. Lehmann, who pioneered in cheap merchandise,
had the true department-store idea as early as 1875, when
he opened "The Fair"—"Everything for Everybody Under One Roof." Other low-priced stores included the
Boston Store; Hillman's; Siegel, Cooper; and Rothschild's,
later bought by Field's and renamed the Davis Store. Maurice Rothschild's and The Hub are men's clothing stores,

and Henry C. Lytton did not relinquish control of the latter until after he had passed his hundredth birthday. Nor must it be forgotten that in addition to being a metropolitan city, Chicago is also a congeries of small towns, each with its own shopping center, so that one often hears a lower-middle-class Chicagoan say, "I haven't been in the Loop in years." Many of these stores have a distinctive character. John M. Smyth's on the West Side is credited with originating time payments, which may be true so far as furniture stores are concerned, though Cyrus McCormick was selling his reapers on the installment plan as early as 1851, and never sued a farmer.

V

A "semi-public school," as Professor Pierce calls it, was opened by a Miss Eliza Chappel on South Water Street in 1833. The Chicago school system goes back to 1838, but for a long time its provisions were more honored in the breach than in the observance, and the average term of attendance was not more than six weeks. The teaching of music, which, along with other marginal subjects, has caused considerable controversy during Chicago history, began at the end of 1841, the year before the employment of women teachers was authorized. In 1854, John C. Dore came from Boston to be first superintendent of schools. A coeducational high school was opened in 1856, and this was the only public high school until the eighties, when the North, South, and West Division High schools began. The Catholics, who, like the Lutherans, German Methodists, and others, had a parochial school system of their own, had been more forward-looking here, for they had established what they called St. Mary's College of the Lake for boys in 1844, and this was supplemented in 1847 by St. Francis Xavier's Female Seminary.

Evening schools were set up in 1863 and widely used. Manual training got into the high schools in 1885, and in 1890 a technical and commercial high school was established. Kindergartens began under private auspices and were not taken over by the city until 1892, but there was a school for deaf-mute children as early as 1874. Not only Latin but Greek was taught in high school until 1884, when it was dropped over the protest of the distinguished superintendent, George Howland. The German influence was powerful enough to get German taught, even in the elementary schools, but this aroused considerable antagonism and the opposition of other ethnic groups. There were also, of course, numerous private schools for both boys and girls, notably the Chicago Latin School from 1888.

There was no true public library in Chicago until after the Fire. It was dedicated January 1, 1873, in a water tank at the rear of the Rookery Building at Adams and La Salle. The distinguished William Frederick Poole (of *Poole's Index* fame) was the first librarian, and the first book charged out was *Tom Brown's Schooldays*. This was appropriate, for the new library got off the ground with a gift of about seven thousand volumes to the stricken city by many eminent Victorians, including, besides Thomas Hughes, Tennyson, Carlyle, Disraeli, and the Queen herself. The present building, on Michigan Avenue between Washington and Randolph, was erected at a cost of about two million dollars in 1897. It is distinguished by Cararra marble and green-and-gold mosaic work, and books are checked out under an impressive dome of Tiffany glass, around the base of which may be read Milton's words:

"Many a man lives a burden to the earth, but a good book is the precious life blood of a master spirit, embalmed and treasured up on purpose to a life beyond life." Its branches reach all over the city; in 1960 it reported the number of volumes it possessed as 2,521,106, and its circulation as 10,221,628.

In addition to the libraries maintained by educational institutions, Chicago possesses two other great reference libraries open to the public: Newberry, opened in 1885 (again with Poole as the first librarian) and John Crerar, opened in 1897. Newberry devotes itself to the humanities; both its general and its Chicago area holdings are very important. Crerar concerns itself with the physical, natural, and social sciences.

Literary and other clubs began in Chicago as early as the thirties—the Lyceum in 1834. The Young Men's Association (1841) was interested in both literature and "the formation of Moral Character in all its Soundness and High Excellence." The Mechanics' Institute, the Chicago Horticultural Society, and others followed. The Union League Club began in 1869 and the Woman's Fortnightly in 1873, and 1876 saw the birth of the Chicago Woman's Club, which interested itself particularly in social problems. In 1874 the Literary Club began. In 1905, Rotary was organized in Chicago by Paul Harris and others. The Little Room, a genteel body of writers which took its name from a ghost story by one of its members, Madeleine Yale Wynne, began about 1896, and in 1908, Hamlin Garland organized the Cliff Dwellers. Less exclusive organizations include the Bookfellows, the Society of Midland Authors, the Friends of American Writers, and the Friends of Literature.

The story of the University of Chicago is the most dramatic in the local educational record, if only because it was created out-of-hand and virtually overnight with Standard Oil money, plus a generous gift of land from Marshall Field. You cannot create a great university that way, but the fact remains that William Rainey Harper did it. Between 1857 and 1886 the Baptists had operated an "old" University of Chicago on Stephen A. Douglas's land, but this had now gone under. Later, during the controversial regime of Robert Maynard Hutchins (1929–51), when more educational experiments were tried than even Harper had ever dreamed of, and the university became a center of neo-Thomist interest, the wags were to speak of it as a Baptist institution engaged in teaching Roman Catholic theology to Jewish students.

Harper was an amazing man. Born in the classical log cabin in Ohio, he graduated from college at fourteen with an oration in Hebrew and received his Ph.D. from Yale at eighteen. In 1879 he was teaching Hebrew at Morgan Park Seminary in Chicago; in 1886 he was called to Yale. It may be true, as his biographer, Thomas Wakefield Goodspeed, insists, that he was essentially a scholar and that "business was not his line," but educational promotion was. He popularized the study of Hebrew all over the country, through Chautauqua and summer schools, long before he had ever heard of the University of Chicago, and he began public speaking before he had learned how to speak. In the early days he was interested in linguistics rather than either literature or ideas; he was an evangelist without a message. At Chicago he was professor as well as president, but the fact that he was working seventeen hours a day did not prevent him from taking on the superintendency of the Sunday school at the Hyde Park Baptist Church, the presidency of the Chicago Baptist Ministers' Conference, or the duties of a member of the Board of Education. When, in 1905, he learned that he had been stricken with cancer, he fought it to the last ditch, almost fainted at his final convocation, and worked virtually to the last day of his life. His important commentary on Amos and Hosea in "The International Critical Commentary" and his book, *The Prophetic Element in the Old Testament*, were among his 1905 publications. "Many a considerable reputation," says Goodspeed, "has been built on a smaller output of literary material in a lifetime than this one year saw published."

Harper did not care for sport, yet his attitude toward football at the university was rather childish, and his enthusiasm for the Spanish-American War was worse than that. His recreations were cycling and playing the cornet. His heavy schedule of budgeted time left him little leisure for social life, but he made it his business to become acquainted with and show an interest in even graduate assistants, and when there was illness or trouble in a faculty family, he was always there. He never discharged a man for ideological differences, and he always showed mercy where mercy was possible. "The university can stand it," he was quoted as saying; "the man cannot."

Classes began on October 1, 1892. Harper, working until late the night before, wondered if a single student would appear. There were 540, 128 of them graduate students. At twelve-thirty there were simple exercises in Cobb Hall —hymns, Scripture, and prayer; there was no speaking.

Salaries for full professors were first set at $6,000, then raised to $7,000, which was very high for the period. The teaching load was eight to ten hours a week, which was very low. Nine college presidents, including the president of the University of Wisconsin, gave up their administrative posts to teach under Harper; he took fifteen scientists, including A. A. Michelson and Jacques Loeb, from Clark University at a single swoop. It began to be said that the highest degree an educator could receive was C.T.C. (Called to Chicago).

As Chicago was the first city to have a juvenile court, Harper's was the first large university to have a Department of Sociology. The use of the quarter system made it possible to operate on a regular basis in the summer; students could enter in any one of the four quarters and take any quarter off; there were four convocations a year. University Extension and Publications were organized at the same time as the university proper; a fourth division—Libraries, Laboratories, and Museums—was added later. There was great resistance to the idea of a press—"no American university at that time had one"—but Harper stood firm. The *Journal of Political Economy* was the first periodical established; this was followed by the *Journal of Geology*, the *Biblical World*, and others. The Harper Library was not opened until 1912, as a memorial to the first president, and John D. Rockefeller's last great gift was the magnificent chapel dedicated in 1928.

Northwestern University, Methodist in origin, was chartered by the legislature in 1851 and was first intended to be established at Jackson and La Salle, but shifted to its lake front location on the North Shore, where the village was laid out around the university and named Evanston in honor of Dr. John Evans, first president of the university trustees. Instruction began in 1855. During recent years Northwestern has acquired a tremendous Technological Institute and an impressive downtown campus for its medical and other professional schools in what used to be "Streeterville," the area which, until 1918, Chicago's most picturesque squatter, Captain George Washington Streeter,

53

thought to maintain as "the District of Lake Michigan," independent of both Chicago and Illinois. Two years after the first classes met in Evanston, the Presbyterians opened what has become Lake Forest University farther up the North Shore, and in recent years Roosevelt University, which grew out of a revolt against Central YMCA College, has developed in the Auditorium building with the aid of Marshall Field III. The Jesuit university, Loyola, with its regular campus in Rogers Park, grew out of St. Ignatius College, established on the West Side in 1869, where the younger Carter Harrison was educated. De Paul University is operated by the Order of St. Vincent. Cardinal Mundelein gave a great impetus to Catholic education in the Chicago area, fostering Rosary College in River Forest, under the direction of a company of Dominican nuns from Sinsinawa, Wisconsin, and Mundelein College, under that of the Sisters of Charity of the Blessed Virgin. In 1920, the diamond jubilee year of the diocese, Mundelein revealed his plans for a major seminary at Libertyville on the shores of Lake Area, and Libertyville changed its name to Mundelein. But even a brief account of all the educational institutions of the Chicago area would be a book in itself, for the city is one of the great educational centers of the world and one of the great medical centers of the world. Chartered in 1837 and opened in 1844, Rush was the first medical college west of Ohio. The Goldblatt, Wieboldt, and Mandel merchandising families have all been generous givers to medical aid and research, and at present the three great medical centers of Chicago cluster about the Cook County Hospital area on the West Side, Northwestern's downtown campus on the near North Side, and the University of Chicago in Hyde Park.

3

Enemies of Civilization in Chicago

"EARTH might be fair," even in the city. What prevents it? Crime, vice, greed, cruelty and injustice, stupidity and hardness of heart, political corruption, and natural calamity. Chicago has had them all, and they cannot be left out of her story, for we cannot gauge the vitality of her civilization without knowing what it has struggled against and overcome.

I

On Sunday, October 8, 1871, my grandparents were living on the near North Side. My grandfather was hobbling about the house on crutches, having just begun to get the better of a stiff battle with rheumatism. His wife had not set foot out of her bed since the birth of a child late in August.

Grandfather hobbled out to the front door and back into the bedroom.

"You'd better get up," he said, "and get the children dressed. There's a terrible fire, and I'm afraid it's coming this way."

In a few minutes the front door was hot. The two older girls got their clothes on, but my mother, who was two years old, and the baby-in-arms were taken out into the red night in their sleeping clothes.

The family found refuge in the house of friends, but no sooner had they settled down than the fire caught up with them. Three times that night they started out afresh.

Out of grandfather's small earnings in South Water Street they had managed to save eight hundred dollars. In those days humble people did not have bank accounts. My grandmother kept her eight hundred dollars in an old pocketbook. She had a baby to carry herself, and her husband was in no condition to carry anything. She turned the pocketbook over to her oldest daughter, then six years old. As long as she lived, my Aunt Frances remembered how she had clutched that pocketbook through the terror-filled, vandal-ridden night, and heard her mother's anxious voice admonishing her: "Frances, whatever you do, hold on to that pocketbook!"

In the course of the night my grandfather was somehow separated from his family, and the fire, which burned until rain mercifully put it out on Tuesday morning, had been over for days before he found them again. For three days and nights my grandmother sat at the window, watching for him. At last she saw him, hobbling painfully along on his crutches a great way off, and ran out to him. But only the strength and confidence of a friend had saved him from throwing himself into the river, for he believed that all his family had been destroyed.

For twenty-five dollars a month he rented a miserable room in an old basement, where the rats promenaded before the family at high noon. . . .

Few great human calamities come unbidden. Most could be prevented if men would use the brains that they were born with. We call it *The* Chicago Fire, but it was not the only one, and it did not come without warning. Everybody knew that the wooden city—wooden houses, wooden sidewalks elevated above the prairies, wood-paved streets—was a tinderbox; in that parched summer and fall it would have been a miracle if calamity had been averted. There had been big fires in 1839, 1849, and 1857, but their warnings had gone unheeded; there had been another on Saturday night; there was to be still another in 1874, which would find the Board of Fire Underwriters threatening to leave the city because their rules were not being complied with. The big one began on the West Side, in a barn back of the O'Leary cottage on DeKoven Street (I am sorry to have to record that the picturesque legend that Mrs. O'Leary's cow kicked over a lantern is only just that), and it jumped the river twice, destroying nearly 18,000 buildings, making nearly 100,000 people homeless, and causing a property loss of $200,000,000, and did not stop until it got to Fullerton Avenue. One hundred and twenty bodies were recovered from the ruins. The O'Leary cottage did not burn! But on the North Side almost nothing was left standing except Mahlon D. Ogden's mansion on the present site of the Newberry Library and the cottage of a policeman named Bellinger. Both buildings were of wood.

Calamity brings out the best and the worst in human nature. Incredible as it seems, they were shooting down pyromaniacs in Chicago for days after the fire ended. Religious fanatics, attributing their own cruelties to God, saw the city punished for her sins, and a Southern political fanatic offered one hundred bales of hay to reward the O'Leary cow. But in the *Tribune* Medill was crying, "Chicago still exists. She was not a mere collection of stone, and bricks and lumber." The Board of Trade voted unanimously to honor all pre-Fire contracts, and the world outside Chicago, including Chicago's rival cities, responded nobly with food, clothing, and credit. Merchants reopened their stores as soon as they could find a barn or a shed to accommodate them, and a real estate man, W. D. Kerfoot, made himself immortal with the sign, "All gone but wife, children, and energy." When Potter Palmer, his courage shaken for once in his life, thought of pulling out, his beautiful young bride quickly halted him. "Mr. Palmer," she declared, "it's the duty of every Chicagoan to stay here and help rebuild this stricken city!" But nobody was braver than Robert Collyer, preaching, the Sunday after the fire, amid the ruins of his church at Chicago Avenue and Dearborn Street: "We have not lost, first, our geography. Nature called the lakes, the forests, the prairies together in convention long before we were born, and they decided that on this spot a great city would be built." The University of Chicago seal, reproduced on all Press books, still shows a phoenix rising from its ashes.

Oddly enough, less heroic disasters took many more lives. Nearly 300 people perished in September, 1860, when the *Lady Elgin* was rammed by a lumber schooner and sunk. Fred Rice, the steward, rode the breakers in a lifeboat to Waukegan, and heroic rescue efforts were made all along the North Shore. Edward A. Spencer, a student at Garrett Biblical Institute in Evanston, swam out seventeen times to bring half-drowned victims ashore. But Milwaukee counted 350 orphans in a single ward. Ballad singers kept the fame of the *Lady Elgin* alive for decades, and sixty survivors held a get-together as late as 1910.

This was not the only marine disaster of the early days. But it was the sluggish Chicago River that was the scene of the worst water disaster in Chicago's history when, early on Saturday morning, July 24, 1915, the excursion steamer *Eastland*, overloaded with passengers bound on a Western Electric outing, calmly turned over on her side at the

Clark Street bridge and drowned 812 people like rats in a trap.

The Iroquois Theater fire, at the holiday midweek matinee, December 30, 1903, claimed fewer lives than this—not more than six hundred—but since so many of them were children, it seemed even more pitiful. The attraction was a musical extravaganza, *Mr. Bluebeard*, starring Eddie Foy, who behaved heroically, as actors always do on such occasions, but everything went wrong. The scenery was highly inflammable, the asbestos curtain seems to have jammed, a draft carried flames and poisonous gases from the stage out into the auditorium, people jumped from the balconies, and the fire exit doors were locked or opened inwards; here and on the stairs the bodies were piled up like cordwood. It was all over in fifteen minutes or so, and they brought the victims out and stacked them along the curb on Randolph Street and on the tables in a nearby lunch room, turning the toughest reporters in town sick.

Dorsha B. Hayes has related how she came to Chicago with her mother and her slightly older brother on the fatal day, from a small town a hundred miles west, to shop in the big city and to meet her father for a first visit to the theater, and how, after he had with difficulty secured four balcony seats for *Mr. Bluebeard*, her mother decided, for some reason she could not explain, that they must not go. I can match this story. I was not yet four years old when the disaster occurred, and though I could not read, I enjoyed looking at the paper. When my father brought the *Daily News* home that night, I took it from him, spread it out on the floor, and got down on my hands and knees to look at it, old enough to be excited by the terrible news but too young to be really moved. I think the first reports were that something like three hundred had been killed, for I remember my mother saying that perhaps it might be thirty, which would be quite bad enough, but the newspapers always exaggerated. This was when I learned that even mothers did not always guess right and noted the fact for future reference. I might, however, have been much more closely connected with the calamity, for my grandmother and my Aunt Frances, who had lived through the Chicago Fire, very nearly died in this one. My aunt planned to take her mother to the performance and actually went to the theater to buy tickets, but when she reached the lobby, she suddenly changed her mind for no reason at all and turned away. And she was not a woman much given to whim.

The Iroquois Theater fire threw actors out of work and led to new safety regulations for theaters in Chicago and across the world. I have never seen standing room sold in any Chicago theater, nor have I ever attended a performance at which the steel or asbestos curtain was not raised and lowered after each act. But even the safety regulations on the books in 1903 would have averted the disaster if they had been obeyed.

II

Chicago's first official hanging was that of John Stone for the murder of Lucretia Thompson at what is now Twenty-ninth Street and South Parkway on July 10, 1840. Convicted on circumstantial evidence, Stone protested his innocence to the end; and when he was asked if he knew who had committed the crime, he declared, "If I did I would swing before their blood should be upon me." Seventeen years passed before another execution took place, this one on the West Side at Ashland and Jackson, public, like the 1840 entertainment, so that the deterrent power of capital punishment might exercise its full effect. On the whole, I would say that Chicago has cultivated quantity rather than quality in its killings; the gangster slaughter of the twenties and thirties does not really count; there was no mystery about it, and everybody's motives were only too plain. "I do not mean to be at all Pharisaic about Chicago," said G. K. Chesterton. "It has many beauties, including the fine fastidiousness and good taste to assassinate nobody except assassins."

The murder of Dr. Patrick Cronin in 1889 (like Dr. Manette, he was called out to attend a patient), which the young Finley Peter Dunne, not yet the creator of Mr. Dooley, helped to solve, and which involved an organization of Irish patriots known as the Clan-na-Gael, had a sufficient number of classical elements in it so that one might expect it to be better remembered than it is; and the nineties contributed both "Dr." H. H. Holmes and the German sausage maker Adolph Luetgert. Luetgert was suspected of having made his wife into sausages, which did not stimulate the sale of the product. Actually he was not making sausages at the period, but he may well have killed her and disposed of her in his plant. Holmes, who was hanged in Philadelphia in 1895, was Chicago's most successful mass murderer, and nobody knows the number of his victims. His Charles Addams-like "murder castle," complete with all the equipment of which any fictionist ever dreamed, survived in Englewood until after the Century of Progress Exposition, but he himself has not lived in the popular imagination to anything like the extent of that mass killer of rural Indiana, Belle Gunness.

Chicago once contemplated erecting a monument to the Fire, and at the Chicago Historical Society fire relics are still cherished like something holy. If it is a public service to stimulate the imagination, great criminals sometimes perform it as effectively as artists do, and one must at least say for them that it often costs them their lives to do it. If ever a legend of juvenile delinquency lived in Chicago, it was that of the "Car Barn Bandits" of 1903, and if ever youngsters lived a *Great Train Robbery* story (it was the very year of the film), it was they. On an August night, four slum boys robbed a streetcar barn, killing a clerk in the process. One went on to kill a policeman while being captured, then confessed and moved out of the picture. The other three escaped to a cave in the Indiana sand dunes, where they lived on cake and dime novels! Here they were besieged by the law, and a battle ensued. They got away, captured a train, killed the brakeman, ran the locomotive for a few miles, escaped to a cornfield, and surrendered. All but one were hanged.

The one Chicago murder case whose classical stature has never been questioned is that of Nathan F. Leopold, Jr., and Richard Loeb, who, in 1924, murdered fourteen-year-old Bobby Franks for a thrill. I have always said that my two claims to fame are that I graduated from high school with Ernest Hemingway and was initiated into Phi Beta Kappa with Nathan Leopold. The crime was so utterly senseless that I can remember people walking about stony-eyed asking, "*Why* did they do it?" It almost seemed as though human nature was turning into something monstrous before our eyes. The city panted for blood, and there can be no doubt that we should have had it, had not Clarence Darrow persuaded the boys to plead guilty, face trial without a jury, and throw themselves upon the mercy of the court. Darrow was a curious Chicago figure. Though unquestionably a true humanitarian, he was quite capable of defending the indefensible where a good fee was involved, and unbeliever though he was, he was very skillful in invoking the Christian ethic when it served his purposes. In this case I think he was justified by the event. Loeb was murdered in prison, apparently while trying to "proposition" a fellow prisoner, but if any twentieth-century man has proved that repentance, conversion, atonement, and redemption are not merely words in ancient theological books, it is Leopold. During his years in prison he remade his life and his mind. Paroled in 1958, he went, as he had wished, to Puerto Rico, to work as a hospital attendant at ten dollars a month. The Leopold-Loeb case did more than illustrate the strange ethical dividing line that runs all through human life; it also furnished one of the best arguments I know against capital punishment.

So far as morals were concerned, early Chicago probably did not differ notably from any other frontier town. As early as 1838 it was found necessary to clap fines on disorderly houses, and by 1849 there were said to be more gambling hells in proportion to population than in New York. The city's central position brought criminals to town as well as traders, and many of the latter had more money in their pockets than they knew how to dispose of in any respectable fashion. During the Civil War, Mississippi gamblers drifted up the river, and "war widows" took to prostitution, setting up "light housekeeping," and later "parlor houses," on the upper floors of business buildings in the Loop itself. Later, vice tended to segregate itself on the so-called "Levee," in the First Ward; and State and Dearborn streets, south of Van Buren, were open strongholds of sin. Long before this, some of the "madams" had already become figures in the life of the city; by discarding the red window shades and large house numbers previously in vogue, in favor of a neat copper plate engraved with her name, one Lou Harper is said to have begun the trend toward elegance which after 1900 reached its apogee in the famous establishment of the Everleigh sisters at 2131–33 South Dearborn Street. In the seventies Chapin and Gore, restauranteurs and liquor dealers, managed to keep one foot each in two worlds, but Randolph was not the only street given over to wide-open gambling, and the king of the gamblers, "Mike" McDonald, was reckoned a great force in city politics. Charles Hermann, who knew him well, called McDonald "a better man than his reputation indicated," a devoted husband, and a "sucker" who was given "the worst kind of deal" by both of his wives.

For that matter, even the "Lords of the Levee," as Wendt and Kogan have called them—"Bathhouse John" Coughlin and Michael ("Hinky Dink") Kenna, the First Ward aldermen who wielded enough influence in the City Council so that Carter Harrison II had to have their help when he wanted to smash Yerkes—came to be regarded with a certain retrospective affection after the city had been taken over by the Capone mob in the twenties. "The Bath" rather naïvely admired Harrison, whom he would have liked to see president, with himself as mayor of Chicago. Both he and Kenna grew fat on liquor violations, lust, and graft, and every whore, pimp, and "madam" in town paraded in the drunken saturnalia of the First Ward balls at the Coliseum, but they wanted nothing to do with murder, and when the mobsters moved in, they were as frightened as any decent citizen. Indeed "The Bath" himself had once gone so far as to favor a high license fee for all sellers of cigarettes and prohibit their sale entirely in the immediate vicinity of any school.

"Hinky Dink" was a weazened, morose little man with a code of his own; "The Bath" was a clown whose only real rival in Chicago history was Mayor Thompson. At one of the Coliseum balls he wore a tail coat of billiard-cloth green with a mauve vest, lavender trousers and cravat, yellow pumps, and pale pink kid gloves. He fancied himself the "Poet Lariat of the First Ward," and his masterpiece was "Dear Midnight of Love," which he got little May de Sousa, daughter of a Chicago detective with a respectable stage career before her, to sing at the Chicago Opera House in 1900, after Madame Calvé had turned him down. Among Coughlin's later masterpieces were "Ode to a Bath Tub," "An Ode to a Bowl of Soup," "Suds and Spuds," "Two Thirsts with but a Single Drink," "They're Tearing Up Clark Street Again," and "She Sleeps at the Side of the Drainage Canal." The *Tribune* printed his collected poems in color as a Sunday supplement, but Jack Lait charged that the later ones had been written by one Jack Kelley, who, in 1932, is said to have owned up.

As for alcohol, Chicago had been wet as wet from the beginning, and the liquor interests had never co-operated in the enforcement of any regulatory legislation. Joseph Medill was the only mayor ever elected as a dry, though Thompson, for some reason best known to himself, enforced the state Sunday closing law briefly during his first term, and the heroic and high-minded William E. Dever made an honest effort to carry out the provisions of a prohibition law in which he did not believe. Of course the churches fought both liquor and vice, sometimes with more drama than sense, as when "Gypsy" Smith led a praying crusade into the Levee, and some of his train stayed there after he had gone home. Though professing herself grateful for the business, Minna Everleigh said she was sorry to see "so many young men coming down here for the first time." According to Burton Rascoe, a regular institution of fraternity life at the University of Chicago during his time consisted in raw freshmen, particularly those from the farms and small towns, being escorted to the red light district by their older "brothers," one of the aspects of higher education in America perhaps not sufficiently pondered by those who expatiate on the advantages of "college life" outside the classroom.

The most famous and luxurious and probably the highest-priced brothel in the world, the Everleigh Club was closed by Carter Harrison II in 1911. It has been said that he was angered by the publication of a brochure, depicting interiors which prove that Hollywood has never exaggerated anything in picturing the tasteless haunts of gilded vice. This is too simple an explanation. There had been sporting house directories and even vice district newspapers in Chicago long before this. Harrison was incensed by the vice district's breaking out from its hitherto tacitly recognized boundaries, the demand for reform was in the air, and he did not move against the Everleigh Club alone; before he was through, he had finished segregated vice in Chicago. He also smashed the Washington Park race track, in which many of his critics had an interest, and revoked the licenses of many cafés and saloons. According to legend, manners were very genteel at the Everleigh, where a "never on Sundays" policy prevailed. Harrison did not, however, subscribe to the usual view that Ada and Minna were in themselves the most genteel of ladies, seeing them instead in his memoirs as "painted, peroxided, bedizened," "harridan sisters," "whited ... or rather gaudily bedaubed sepulchres," "caricatures of human kind," "poor, wretched, doddering burlesques of femininity." I have never encountered so many opprobrious epithets applied to a single pair of females in equally limited space.

Between 1879 and 1915 the two Carter Harrisons served
five terms each as mayor of Chicago, and church forces
generally disliked them because they were reputed to run
a wide-open town. Yet both were honorable and lovable
men, and neither was ever even suspected of dishonesty.
In an early campaign, the son, who was as handsome as a
matinee idol, used a picture of himself with his hands in
his pockets and the legend "Chicago is fortunate in having
a mayor who keeps his hands in his own pockets." This
was no empty boast; he was so scrupulous that when his
wife came into his office one day and asked him for stamps
for three letters, he told her that if she really wanted him
to steal from the city, there was no point in stopping with
six cents, for he could get a million dollars just as easily. His
father, a Kentuckian who rode about the city on his blooded
mare, waving his broad-brimmed hat at his constituents
and talking to as many of them as possible, was a picturesque figure indeed. Of course he knew that this was
good politics, but there is abundant evidence that he was
being himself also, for he had a kind and generous heart, as
he proved time and again. Nobody paid for protection under the Harrisons; they simply took it for granted that you
cannot legislate righteousness, and whether they were right
or wrong about this, it may be that they contributed importantly to holding back the flood of corruption that swept
over the city when they were no longer in the picture.
Carter II was never quite as "liberal" as his father, and it
was a bit ironical that he should finally have functioned
so effectively as a reformer, but when he found that he
had not ended prostitution but only scattered it, he must
have wondered whether the old man had not been right
after all. In a sense he got his revenge on all his opponents
when, while he was doing Red Cross work in France after

World War I, the *Tribune* and the *Daily News*, both of which had fought him bitterly, sent an emissary, asking him to save the city from what had befallen her by coming back and standing for mayor again, but he refused.

III

Vice cannot exist without graft, and Chicago has had its share. As early as the seventies the rebuilt county court house was openly described as a thief's monument. In 1917 the Committee of Fifteen declared that 10 per cent of the police were "inherently crooked," and though conditions are now better than they used to be, according to Virgil Peterson and the Crime Commission, crime still costs the city $750,000,000 a year.

The most famous corruptionists in the city's history were probably William Lorimer and Charles T. Yerkes. The son of an English Presbyterian minister, the soft-spoken Lorimer was a model boy—and man, so far as his private conduct was concerned—who first showed his mettle by organizing the Street Railway Employees Benevolent Association. His enemies were the *Tribune* and Herman H. Kohlsaat, and the long controversy ended in 1912, when he was unseated on the charge of having used bribery to buy his place in the United States Senate. It was a great fight while it lasted, with Theodore Roosevelt striking his usual high note by announcing his refusal to attend a luncheon at the Hamilton Club if Lorimer were invited. Yerkes, the original of Dreiser's *Financier* and *Titan*, was a different breed of cat. Yerkes had no political ambitions; he simply bought legislators and aldermen when they got in the way of his enterprises, and when he could not buy Governor Altgeld or Mayor Harrison, his career in Chicago was over. Forrest McDonald has recently defended Yerkes as less the creator of corruption than its victim, and while this seems overcharitable, it must be admitted that the whole traction situation in Chicago was such a mess that probably no man could have handled the franchise situation honestly and managed to stay in business. Yerkes gave a great observatory to the University of Chicago, and he always had the decency to admire those who stood out against him. When he died in 1905, he left only $2,100,000. One day a reporter from one of the scandal papers came to him with an article about his wife. Print anything you like about me, said Yerkes, and I will do nothing. But tell your editor that if he prints one word about my wife, I will shoot him dead within twenty-four hours. It is difficult to avoid admiring this, and if such admiration comes under the head of condoning murder, I can only reply that I am not sure the commandment covers vermin.

Lorimer was allied with Yerkes, and William Hale Thompson in his early days was Lorimer's protégé. They were an unholy trinity. Of Thompson a contemporary observer remarked that "he has given the city an international reputation for moronic buffoonery, barbaric crime, triumphant hoodlumism, unchecked graft and a dejected citizenship. He nearly ruined the property and completely destroyed the pride of the city. He made Chicago a by-word of the collapse of American civilization." Thompson was such a clown that he would have been a disgrace to Chicago even if he had not turned it over to the mobsters. Oddly enough, he was born on Boston's Beacon Street in 1867, and began his career as a hard-riding, hard-drinking cowboy on a Wyoming ranch. Back in Chicago, he became known as an all-star athlete and entered politics as a reform alderman, backed by the lily-white Civic Federation!

In his first campaign he promised lower streetcar fares,

improved garbage collections, and better schools. Elected, he ordered the chief of police to drive every crook out of the city in sixty days and bolstered his prestige by settling a streetcar strike. But in the first four months of his administration, ten thousand "temporary employees" were added to the city payroll to pay off his political debts.

Thompson appointed Al Capone's agent city sealer. He ousted the superintendent of schools because he was using pro-British books and started a drive to eliminate similar contaminated material from the Public Library. "I wanta make the King of England keep his snoot out of America!" In foreign wards he complained that the Revolutionary War heroes of various ethnic groups were being played down, but it was noted that he sometimes called them "Pulasko" and "Kosciuski." Yet when he campaigned against Cermak, he was quite capable of twitting "Tony" with his Czech origin and urging him to go back to his pushcart. He carried caged rats to his political rallies and addressed them by the names of his enemies. He reduced immigrant women to hysterics by telling them that the schools which the present mayor had constructed were going to collapse and kill all their children and that the mayor had men working every night to cover up the cracks in the arches. "I hope to God these arches hold up until election day."

Did he do anything right? This is a hard question to ask or to answer about any politician, for politics is a confused business. Judge Edward F. Dunne was a fine man, who was elected mayor of Chicago to achieve municipal ownership of the traction lines, but he surrounded himself with starry-eyed idealists like himself and accomplished little. On the other hand, Fred A. Busse was a coarse man with friends who were considerably worse than that, but he appointed the Vice Commission, launched the Chicago Plan, and made Ella Flagg Young superintendent of schools. And though Cermak himself was no prize, the better elements in the city finally rallied around him almost unanimously as the only hope of getting rid of Thompson.

Thompson published a pamphlet called *Eight Years of Progress* in which he listed among his achievements 89 streets widened, 832 miles of streets paved, 402 miles of sewers constructed, 55 new playgrounds established, the Michigan Avenue bridge completed, a fish hatchery established in Lincoln Park, two Pageants of Progress held. Some of these achievements were genuine, though he neglected to mention how much more they had all cost than would have been necessary. Personally, however, I am more interested in the fact that, in a city gone mad with World War I fever, except for the *Tribune*, Thompson's was the only voice raised in favor of any degree of tolerance for dissenters. Of course he was boorish and oafish in his attitude toward General Joffre's visit, but when, in September, 1917, he allowed a pacifist group to hold a meeting in Chicago while Governor Lowden was rushing troops from Springfield to chase them out, it was the oaf and not the gentleman by whom the American tradition was upheld. Thompson was such a confused creature that his motives are always hard to fathom. Obviously he was fishing for the German vote, but he must also have known that he was antagonizing the American vote. He seems to have been as sincere about peace as he was capable of being about anything. He had proposed an embargo on war materials as early as 1915, and as late as 1937 he formed a William Hale Thompson Association to Keep America Out of Foreign Wars and actually got a proposition on the ballot calling upon congressmen to enact legislation prohibiting draft of American manpower for service abroad. In a year in which no single Republican was elected in Cook County, 1,700,000 Illinoisans voted "yes" to 958,000 "no's."

This is not the place to tell the story of the beer barons and their wars, of Al Capone, who came to Chicago as a district captain under Johnny Torrio, who afterwards cleared out and left the racket to him, of the killing of Jim Colosimo, Dion O'Banion, Hymie Weiss, and the rest, or of the hideous St. Valentine's Day massacre of 1929. After Dever became mayor of Chicago, the strategy involved the capture by the gangsters of the once decent town of Cicero, which Capone ruled, virtually like a conquered city, from his armored headquarters at the Hawthorne Inn. By 1934, Chicago even seemed the right place for federal agents to shoot down "Public Enemy Number One" John Dillinger, as he emerged from the Biograph Theater on the North Side, where I had once upon a time gone on Saturday afternoons to see revivals of Mary Pickford films. But the really shocking thing is the fact that even when the law got the big mobster at last and put him behind the bars, it was only on an income tax charge that they toppled him, and the hideous doubt intrudes whether the improvement in conditions since has really been effected by either the authorities or an outraged citizenry, or whether it has not merely followed from the operation of changing social forces.

Gangsters had appeared in Chicago before prohibition; the Hearst forces employed the Annenbergs to destroy *Tribunes* and intimidate those who sold them in the early days of their newspaper enterprises there, and the *Tribune* had "protected" itself until James Keeley got Max Annenberg himself to come over to the *Tribune*, where he ultimately became respectable and proved himself a mighty circulation builder. From here on, "protection" was extended to other enterprises and industries.

The most disgusting thing of all, however, is that Chicago once seemed to take pride in Capone and his kind; Colosimo's funeral was attended by two judges, three aldermen, a former assistant district attorney, and a bailiff of the municipal court. Mary Borden, revisiting Chicago in 1931, when Capone was operating a soup kitchen for the unemployed, was nauseated by "a lovely member of Chicago's four hundred" who could not speak of the gangster without tears of admiration. Yet Capone himself was a sentimentalist, as many immoralists are. At the Lexingon Hotel, where he lived, he had framed portraits of his three favorite Americans—Washington, Lincoln, and William Hale Thompson—and when Ethel Barrymore brought Sierra's beautiful play *The Kingdom of God* to Chicago, he sat in the first row, holding his wife's hand throughout the performance, with the tears streaming down his face.

Yet there have been efforts to clean house in various aspects, and some of them have done some good. Raids go clear back to 1857, when Mayor "Long John" Wentworth went into "The Sands" and literally pulled the wretched buildings down, a method better calculated to gratify sadistic impulses than achieve any permanent reform. After W. T. Stead's exposure in *If Christ Came to Chicago* (1894), the Civic Federation was formed, whose subsidiary, the Municipal Voters League, headed by a dauntless, stocky, and pugnacious stationer named George E. Cole, exposed corruption and corruptionists as they had never been exposed in Chicago, and showing what an aroused citizenry can accomplish toward cleaning the boodlers out if it really cares to take the trouble. Mayor Busse's Vice Commission was equally specific; incidentally, it estimated the annual profits of organized vice in Chicago at $15,000,000 and bravely attacked economic injustice as a contributing factor. When the New Testament scholar, Ernest DeWitt Burton, president-to-be of the University of Chicago, read it, he declared, "I ought not to be sitting here reading this. I ought to be out killing somebody."

IV

But the most famous Chicago calamity except the Fire—and the most controversial of all—had nothing to do with gangsters. Strictly speaking, the Haymarket Riot of May 4, 1886, was not a riot, and it occurred on Desplaines Street, between the Haymarket and the alley which runs east from Desplaines. The occasion was a protest meeting growing out of a strike at the McCormick Reaper works; because the weather was threatening, it was not largely attended; though it was addressed by wild-eyed anarchists, they were, for them, comparatively restrained. Mayor Harrison had been present, and before he went home had stopped at the police station to assure those in charge that no action was called for. Then, a few minutes before everything would have been over, a brutal police captain, John Bonfield, decided to go in and crack a few heads; before he could achieve this ambition, a bomb was thrown by an unknown hand.

Eight men were tried for their lives. Of the seven sentenced to death, four were hanged (November 12, 1887), one committed suicide, and the other sentences were commuted to imprisonment. The case became a world-wide *cause célèbre* not because people had any sympathy with anarchists but because the judge had shown obvious prejudice, the jury was packed, and the sentence was not in accord with Anglo-Saxon principles of justice. None of the men tried were even accused of having thrown the bomb, and since the actual criminal was never apprehended, there was no possibility of proving that he had been influenced by them.

The only possible excuse for Chicago is that she was scared stiff, but as George Bancroft once declared, "the fears of one class of men are not the measure of the rights of another." My mother used to tell me that on the day of the hangings she was afraid to go down town because people believed that the anarchists were going to blow up the city. There were hardly enough of them to count, but they had done their best to make people believe that this did not matter. Most of them were German, but Albert R. Parsons was a Confederate war veteran of *Mayflower* stock, who had married a lady of color. He escaped from the city after the fatal night, then voluntarily appeared in court and took his place with his comrades. Listen to him on the subject of dynamite: "It is democratic; it makes everybody equal. The Pinkertons, the police, the militia, are absolutely worthless in the presence of dynamite. . . . It is the disseminator of authority; it is the dawn of peace; it is the end of war. It is man's best and last friend; it emancipates the world from the domineering of the few over the many, because all government, in the last resort, is violence; all law, in the last resort, is force."

Of course, it was insane, though I doubt that any of those who put their hope of world peace in the atom bomb have a right to think so. Nor is it fair to consider such utterances without reference to the hideous labor injustices which prevailed in those days, or such incidents as the 1877 outrage at the West Side Turner Hall, when police broke in upon a peaceful meeting discussing the eight-hour day, clubbed the participants, and killed one of them. When the case came up before Judge McAllister, he bravely told the men that they would have been within their legal rights if they

had killed every policeman on the spot. One of the anarchists, August Spies, told Victor Dennis of the *Daily
News:* "If the newspapers would report our speeches when
we use moderate language we should not be forced to talk
of dynamite and revolution." He was a fool, for the kind of
reporting the newspapers gave violent speeches did the anarchists no good, and the Haymarket tragedy set back the
cause of labor in America for many years. As late as 1907,
when Jack London wrote *The Iron Heel*, he chose Chicago
as the fittest setting for a violent revolution.

That unusual banker, Lyman J. Gage, one of the finest
citizens in Chicago's history, regretted the Haymarket convictions; so did Marvin Hughitt, president of the Northwestern Railroad; so did Potter Palmer, who had Quakerism
in his background. Governor Oglesby promised to com-
mute the death sentences if the leading citizens of Chicago
requested it. Gage called fifty men to a meeting, and they
would probably have voted as he desired if Marshall Field
had not opposed him. Field had already done his part to
save the city by persuading the Commercial Club to give
the government the 632 acres which became Fort Sheridan;
not to be outdone, the Merchants Club gave the land for
the Great Lakes Naval Training Station. Encouraged by
world-wide protest and undaunted by his neighbors, Gage
established an open forum for the discussion of public questions from which no shades of opinion were barred, but
regretfully reported that the meetings were "attended but
feebly by the well-to-do people." He would not call them
the "higher classes"; "self-satisfied," he thought, was better.

The shock of the Haymarket executions made young
Emma Goldman an anarchist; on the fatal day, the *Daily
News* sold 482,843 copies, an increase of 180 per cent over

the normal sale. Four foolish men were buried under an impressive monument in Waldheim Cemetery, with a bronze statue of an angry-looking woman, protecting a dying man from his enemies and placing a wreath of laurel on his brow. "The day will come," promised the legend, "when our silence will be more powerful than the voices ye are throttling today."

This was not the only tragedy of its kind that Chicago has known, though it was certainly the most spectacular. In the same period there was the collapse of George M. ("Sleeping Car") Pullman's model town, the fulfillment of his childhood desire to "do something for humanity," which caused Jane Addams to liken him to King Lear, and may well have killed him. The workman's obligations to the town of Pullman were taken out of his pay check; if there was nothing left, that was none of Pullman's business, even if he had just ordered a wage cut. When the finally disastrous strike came, he snubbed both Lyman Gage and Mrs. Palmer in their efforts to arbitrate. "Go and live in Pullman and find out how much Pullman gets sellin' city water and gas ten per cent higher to those poor fools!" cried Mark Hanna. "A man who won't meet his own men half-way is a God-damn fool!" And so the Pullman utopia, like so many others, was wrecked on the rock of its own designer's intransigence.

More disgraceful still were the terrible race riots of 1919. During World War I, Negroes swarmed into Chicago from the South to fill up the labor shortage, taking possession of such once-proud streets as Grand Boulevard, South Park Avenue, and Prairie Avenue, and the shattered mansions of the old Levee, where, it is said, they came upon decayed, rich costumes, tunnels, strange electrical devices, and sometimes a skeleton. Thompson wooed and won them—and the Negro vote became an important element in his fortunes—but he fed them nothing but windy words.

During the two years preceding July, 1919, there had been twenty-four bombings directed against Negroes. On the twenty-seventh a Negro boy swam into the white area at a South Side bathing beach and was stoned and drowned. This outrage set off five days of rioting (complicated by a streetcar strike) in which thirty-eight persons were killed and more than five hundred injured, with more than two million dollars in property damage. Negro help disappeared temporarily from Chicago hotels; an actor appearing in a Loop theater saved a Negro who fled into a stage alley by taking him in through the stage door after which he hid and fed him backstage for two days.

v

The last subject to be considered in this chapter does not belong here. When Edgar Lee Masters said that Samuel Insull was a greater enemy of Chicago than Al Capone, he was indulging in the kind of hysteria that renders all moralistic judgments suspect. Capone was a wrecker. Insull was a builder, one of the greatest the country has known. He electrified the Middle West—and charged less for it than almost any other man would have done. His labor relations were good; he pioneered in developing the big corporation owned by a multitude of small stockholders. Oddly enough, he was a radical in his way, and he anticipated some of F.D.R.'s own ideas concerning the relationship between business and government.

Not that one could ever have suspected this during the 1932 campaign, when Roosevelt, who had an old score to settle with Insull, made political capital of the fallen lion, with his famous references to "the Ishmaels and the Insulls, whose hand is against every man," until he reached Chicago, where, learning that Mayor Cermak, who had opposed him in the convention and whose support he was trying to win, was on the other side, he hastily altered his projected speech. "I have committed no crime," declared the aging financier, when the Roosevelt government, determined to crucify him as a symbol of the old order, used extralegal pressure to bring him back from Europe to his trial in Chicago. "The failure of my companies was not fraudulent. I have just been unfortunate and lost lots of money—more than $100,000,000 of my own." But the government's case against him was based on Insull's own records, and the jury, unable to believe that a crook could keep honest records, earn over half a million a year and give still more than that away, or ruin himself along with those whom he had "defrauded," took less than five minutes to decide that Insull was innocent, and then sat down and "killed" two hours before bringing in their verdict, lest they should be suspected of having been bribed. The mountain had labored and brought forth a mouse—except for the "smear" and the smell, which are still with us.

Born in London in 1859, the son of a lay preacher and temperance worker (he was himself a lifelong teetotaler), Insull came to America in 1881 to work for Edison. In 1892 he arrived in Chicago, just in time for the electrical display at the World's Columbian Exposition; by 1907 he was head of Commonwealth Edison and in supreme control of the electrical business of the city. In 1910 he extended his business outside Chicago into what became the Public Service Company of Northern Illinois, supplying cheap power to scores of hitherto unelectrified communities. This led in turn to Middle Western Utilities, and before he was through

Insull was supplying not only electricity but gas, water, ice, and heat to some four thousand towns from Maine to Texas. In Chicago he also controlled the Peoples Gas Light and Coke Company and the elevated railroad, with its inter-urban extensions, north, south, and west. These he took on not because he wanted them but because he was appealed to in an attempt to keep them running.

Insull's courage was dauntless, and his daring imagina-tion failed him only when it was required to envisage dis-aster. Even after the stock market crash he continued to assume new burdens up to $200,000,000. He guaranteed the accounts of employees who had been caught short, saved a long list of businesses, and practically took over the city payroll. Even at the end, it was Insull's enemies, rather than Insull, who brought his house down around his ears; the pyramiding, debt financing, etc. into which he suffered himself to be led were desperate attempts to meet a situation which had been forced upon him. But if those who at last made a bankrupt of him had had half his sand or half that of his son (who had to be left to face the music in Chicago while his father hid out in Europe), the outcome might well have been different, and if the bankers had had sense enough to protect their own investments, the House of Insull might still have weathered the storm.

None of this is to be interpreted as a blanket endorsement of everything Insull did; that some of his policies were un-wise was proved by the event, but the whole financial world was in it with him up to the neck, and if he had not failed, no whisper would ever have been heard against him. Insull was not a corruptionist, but he had his ties with both Roger Sullivan and the Thompson machine, and he had no hesi-tation about using his money to influence public policy. He was in World War I long before the country, and the power he developed over public opinion and behavior as chairman of the State Council of Defense was frightening. Like everything else he touched, the Council showed a profit, so that people said if he were placed in charge of the war, he could make it pay dividends. It seems odd, incidentally, in view of his devotion to England, that he should, in later years, have been isolationist even to the extent of opposing the World Court.

There was never any halfway house about Insull; people either loathed him or followed him to the death. Chicago society in general disliked him, calling him rude and being disquieted by his penetrating eyes and unintentionally sneering lip, and he paid them back when he built the great Civic Opera House without a golden horseshoe, with the boxes tucked away decorously under the balcony, like the mezzanine floor in a great motion picture "palace." It was a costly error. "All power corrupts, and absolute power corrupts absolutely." Because Insull was a human being, he could be tyrannical, benevolently and nonbenevolently also. But his telephone number was in the book; anybody in Chicago could talk to him at will; he preferred helping needy individuals to putting his money into foundations, and there must have been few who ever appealed to him in vain.

4

Instead of focusing on topics, like the preceding chapters, this chapter and the next will describe various Chicago activities as expressions of the people who participated in them. Be it clearly understood that the title of this chapter is not "The Five Greatest Chicagoans." I have not even said that these are the five Chicagoans whom I consider greatest in their respective lines. In short, I have simply selected five representative figures who would allow me to organize important representative activities about them.

I

Of the political leaders of Chicago and Illinois, who seems at this date most worthy to be remembered? After he pardoned the Chicago anarchists, and even more after his controversy with President Cleveland over the sending of federal troops into Chicago at the time of the Pullman strike, the press of the nation (not merely of Chicago) denounced John Peter Altgeld (1847–1902) as himself an anarchist, a menace to American institutions, almost a red devil. When Vachel Lindsay paid him his famous memorial tribute, he saw fit to call it "The Eagle That Is Forgotten," and the only comfort he could find for the oblivion that had unjustly overtaken a great and good man was that "to live in mankind is far more than to live in a name." But poets are the unacknowledged legislators of mankind, and it was not long before the eagle in question began to look surprisingly like a phoenix.

Altgeld was not a saint; he was a poor immigrant boy who made good in a fiercely competitive world; the builder of the Unity Block hungered for power as well as wealth, and he knew what he had to do to get it. "If I talked as radical as I feel, I could not be where I am. I want to do something, not just make a speech. . . . I want power, to get hold of the handle that controls things. When I do, I will give it a twist!" He "talked radical" enough nevertheless, and though he had no left-wing connections, he sufficiently appealed to the class conflict so that the opposition he awakened becomes credible though not rational. As a politician Altgeld was never corrupt. He is known to have turned down a huge bribe to refrain from vetoing Yerkes' "Eternal Monopoly" bills and to have rejected an Ogden Gas Company "deal," though the acceptance of either offer would have saved him from financial disaster. Yet he operated a spoils system, playing a devious game with great skill and, like the Harrisons, taking his allies where he found them. Even Jane Addams, who admired him, thought he had marred his pardon message by allowing a personal animus to the trial judge, Joseph Gary, to seep into it. There was a vindictive strain in Altgeld, despite all his nobility. It showed when he unfairly attacked the *Tribune* on a tax issue. It showed in the brilliantly organized coup by which he ended John A. Roche's career as mayor of Chicago because he believed Roche had treated him unfairly in a suit against the city. The storms which followed his pardon message and his controversy with Cleveland "finished" Altgeld in the sense that he was never elected to public office afterwards, but in the meantime he had taken his revenge by "finishing off" the President. Under his leadership, the Democratic convention of 1896 in Chicago virtually repudiated Cleveland and adopted a platform dictated by Altgeld, denouncing federal encroachment and government by injunction, championing free silver, arbitration of labor disputes, and a federal income tax. I know of no parallel overthrow in American politics. It is true that Altgeld would have preferred Bland to Bryan as the nominee and that the Democrats were defeated in November (though with Altgeld himself as candidate for re-election as governor, running ten thousand ahead of the national ticket), but none of this lessened either Cleveland's humiliation or the fact that it was Altgeld (not Cleveland, not Bryan) who emerged from the convention as the most powerful man in the party and its intellectual leader.

Yet I myself admire Altgeld most not because he succeeded but because he failed. In pardoning the anarchists, he did not act quickly or hastily, and it is clear that he fought a bitter battle with himself before winning the victory. "I have not yet examined the record," he told the impatient Clarence Darrow. "I have no opinion about it. It is a big job. When I do examine it, I will do what I believe to be right, no matter what that is." But he did not wish Darrow to deceive himself as to the consequences, and he would not let him deceive Altgeld either: "If I conclude to pardon those men, it will not meet with the approval that you expect. Let me tell you . . . from that day, I will be a dead man!"

Many Americans have applauded Henry Clay's "I would rather be right than be President," but few of these have ever been called upon to make the choice. It is good for the American people and for American character that at least one well-known political figure should have deliberately committed political suicide in the interest of conscience. For that example alone John Peter Altgeld has larger claims upon our forbearance than he has ever had need to exercise.

But Altgeld's public service was not limited to the areas already indicated. Laying the cornerstone of the Chicago Academy of Sciences in 1893, he showed a true understanding of what makes for greatness in a city. "The generations to come," he declared, "will care nothing for our warehouses, our buildings or our railroads, but they will ask, what has Chicago done for humanity, where has it made man wiser or nobler or stronger; what new thought or principles or trust has it given to the world?" Altgeld was one of the builders of Lincoln Park. He was the first governor to think of the University of Illinois in big university terms, not the "cow college" terms that had hitherto prevailed. As early as 1884, when he published *Our Penal Machinery and its Victims*, he began his work in behalf of a new criminology, opposing brutality, urging not merely punishment but cure. He argued for the obligation of the state to feed the hungry long before it was generally accepted, and even his old enemies on the *Tribune* supported his campaign to relieve the victims of the Pullman strike after George Pullman himself had washed his hands of them. He urged labor to organize and demand its rights, but he warned that unless the move was made along strictly lawful lines, all would be in vain. He used force promptly and effectively to maintain order in labor disputes as in other sources of turmoil, but he consistently maintained that the function of the troops ended there. You are not soldiers in battle, he told them, and it is your job to "protect life and property *without killing anybody*" if this can possibly be done. "*A soldier . . . becomes a murderer if he needlessly kills.*"

It was fitting that his last speech should have been made in behalf of the embattled Boers: "I am not discouraged. Things will right themselves. The pendulum swings one way and then the other. But the steady pull of gravitation is toward the center of the earth. Any structure must be plumb if it is to endure or the building will fall. So it is with nations. Wrong may seem to triumph. Right may seem to be defeated. But the gravitation of eternal justice is upward toward the throne of God. Any political institution if it is to endure must be plumb with that line of justice."

When he was dead, his body lay in state in the north corridor of the Chicago Public Library, and fifty thousand people stood on Michigan Avenue in a cold March rain to get in and look for the last time on the face of the man whom the newspapers had called the Nero of the late nineteenth century.

II

Philip D. Armour may not have been the packer who vowed to use every part of the pig but his squeal, but he was certainly the most lovable and picturesque of the lot. He came of Revolutionary War stock, first of Connecticut, then of Stockbridge, New York, where he was born on May 16, 1823. He went west and tried mining, then to Milwaukee in the soap business, then to St. Paul and back to Milwaukee. He married a Cincinnati girl and went into packing with a Pennsylvanian named John Plankinton. Foreseeing the end of the Civil War, he sold pork "short" and cleared between $500,000 and $1,500,000. From 1875 on he was in Chicago.

The limitations of the classical type of American businessman can be well illustrated by reference to Armour. He once remarked that his culture was largely in his wife's

86

name, and it was said of him, probably inaccurately, that *David Harum* was the only book he had ever read. But he was himself quite frank about his limitations: "I have no other interest in life but my business. . . . I do not love the money. What I do love is the getting of it. All these years of my life I have put into this work, and now it is my life and I cannot give it up. What other interest can you suggest to me? I do not read. I do not take any part in politics. What can I do?"

Look at the by-products which came out of packing. Ultimately they included toilet soaps and perfumes, medicines and hospital accessories, fertilizers, gelatin and pepsin, violin bows, glue, tallow, and neat's-foot oil. Armour looked forward to manufacturing shoes and clothing, and his company was on the verge of becoming a universal food and drug business when the federal government intervened. But the prime motive behind all this experimentation was not greed but a zeal for production and a constitutional detestation of waste. The bulk of Armour's income always came from meat, and that too was the way he wanted it. "Through the wages I disburse and the provisions I supply, I give more people food than any other man alive."

P. D. was more than a packer; he was also the founder of Armour Institute, which filled an important place in the educational life of Chicago from 1893 until, in 1939, it was merged with Lewis Institute (a West Side liberal arts college founded by the real estate speculator Allan G. Lewis) to form Illinois Institute of Technology, the M.I.T. of the Middle West. It was born of a sermon, "If I Had a Million Dollars," by Armour's pastor, Frank W. Gunsaulus, at the Plymouth Congregational Church. What Gunsaulus would do with a million dollars would be to found a technical institute for boys. It was probably the most immediately effective sermon on record; before he left the building, Armour told Gunsaulus that if he meant what he said and would give five years to the project, he would give him the money.

The inciting force was less an interest in technology than in young people. Armour had already put much time and money into the Armour Mission, which had been founded by his late brother Joseph and had developed trade school aspects. At the height of his power he would play with strange children in the street, and it was while he was frolicking in the snow with his own grandchildren near his Prairie Avenue home that he took the chill which caused his death. He died, January 6, 1901, with the Lord's Prayer on his lips, and two thousand children, white and black, gathered at the Mission to sing his favorite hymns.

Armour got up at five every morning and reached the Yards at seven. He always carried one hundred dollars in his wallet, so that he would have money to give away when he needed it. He did not drink alcohol because he had "cyclones within that would make the engine run wild" if he did. He attended no theater and joined no club, and he would not travel on Sunday if he could avoid it. One night Marshall Field invited him to take a hand at cards. He refused, not because he thought cards wicked but because nine o'clock was his bedtime. "I have not broken my retiring hour for Mrs. Armour, and I see no reason to do it for you."

Yet he was no Pharisee and no prude. Once he gave a clergyman in the Yards district two hundred dollars to see a poor woman who was totally unknown to him through her confinement. When the clergyman learned that the woman was unmarried and tried to return the money, P. D. nearly threw him out of his office. To his commonsensical mind it seemed that a woman without a husband needed more—not less—help than another. He sent Frank Billings, one of the most distinguished physicians in Chicago, to look after her, and when her ordeal was over, he sent her to secretarial school, thus providing her with the means of supporting her child. "A man who will abuse a woman is no good for anything."

During the Panic of 1893 he stopped a run on the Illinois Trust and Savings Bank, in which he had an interest, by the simple expedient of walking along the line of persons come to withdraw their savings. "This bank is all right," he told them. "Bring your checks to my office if you like, and I'll cash every one of 'em there." He cashed more than a thousand checks, and the bank stood firm.

Was this man one of the "robber barons" of American industry, of whom we have heard so much during recent years? He had his "views," hated Altgeld, for example, because he thought him inimical to his interests, but though he contributed heavily to campaign funds, he made no direct attempts to influence public opinion or legislation. Nor did he "pressure" those who came within his circle of influence. "If the next twenty-five years make Armours impossible," he told Gunsaulus, "I want these young people prepared for it. Don't ever let me or my business get in the way of it." He declared without qualification that he had never bribed any man. "When my meats cannot stand the test of any fair and honest inspection bill, I will go out of business."

The meat scandals of the Spanish-American War cannot be judged fairly by a layman at this distance. Armour's biographers insist that "there was no evidence to show that the Powell treated beef ever got beyond the one experiment seen by Major Daly. No chemical treatment was traced to any packer in any of the testimony given. 'Embalmed beef' became a macabre myth, a ghost that never was a corpse." Yet it is clear that it was not a sanitary war and that conditions at the Chicago Stock Yards and elsewhere, later to be exposed by Upton Sinclair *(The Jungle)* and others, were appalling, judged by modern standards.

If P. D. failed anywhere, it was with his son, J. Ogden, who was a totally different kind of man. He never really wanted to be a packer, but P. D. "told him to be at the Yards in his working clothes at seven on Monday morning." For many years he seemed justified by the event. Under J. Ogden Armour the business soared to undreamed-of heights, so that he used to wonder whether he did not have more power than any other man in the world. But his failure paralleled his father's first great extraordinary success, for he did not foresee or adjust to the end of World War I, and as a result he is said to have dropped a million dollars a day for 150 days. By the end of 1922 he had resigned and placed his fortune in the hands of his creditors. The Armours had lost control of the company, and J. Ogden was at last free to live in England, as he had always desired. He died in a London hotel in 1927.

III

Julius Rosenwald earned his money very differently from the Armours. He was born in Springfield, Illinois, August 12, 1862, the son of a German-Jewish immigrant. He began his career working in his father's store and selling pamphlets at the dedication of the Lincoln monument in Springfield. In 1879 he went to New York to work for his uncle in the clothing business, and in 1884 he and his brother started a business of their own. The next year he came to Chicago.

In 1895 he bought a one-quarter interest in Sears, Roebuck and Company for $37,500. The company's reputation at this time was none too good. Sears was a shrewd operator. In 1889 he had advertised "An Astonishing Offer" of an "Upholstered Parlor Set" in the rural weeklies at ninety-five cents. Though the word "miniature" did appear in fine print, farmers were indignant when they received doll furniture, and the Post Office Department considered prosecution. There was also an electric belt sold to cure rheumatism but more successful in burning the patient. Rosenwald insisted on all goods being accurately described and also ended the sale of revolvers and ammunition.

By 1898 the Sears catalogues contained 1,206 pages and included much miscellaneous information and advice. In the Far West their arrival was often signalized by a "catalogue party," and sometimes they were even used as textbooks. Some people wrote Dorothy Dix for personal advice, and some wrote to Sears, Roebuck. But the firm encountered much opposition from local merchants, who in some cases threatened to boycott papers which accepted Sears advertisements and paid bonuses for catalogues to be destroyed. At one time orders were shipped in plain boxes to avoid rousing local prejudices against the customer.

Roebuck retired from the business in 1895 and interested himself in motion picture projectors and Florida real estate; having lost his fortune in the collapse of the Florida boom in 1933, he came back to work for his old firm in a minor capacity. Sears sold out in 1909 for ten million dollars, and Rosenwald became president.

Rosenwald was the prime benefactor of the Negro race in his time. His interest in Negroes was roused by Booker T. Washington's autobiography, *Up from Slavery*, one of the most influential books he ever read. Local influences toward humanitarianism stemmed from Jane Addams and his rabbi, Emil G. Hirsch. He gave a luncheon for Washington at the Blackstone Hotel in 1911, the first such function to be held there for a Negro guest-of-honor. In 1910 he offered $25,000 for a YMCA building for Negroes in any city in which $75,000 more could be raised locally. By 1913 thirteen cities had responded. Sometimes these buildings furnished the only places where Negroes could stop and enjoy recreational facilities; in Dallas the enterprise was said to have signalized the first joint effort of Negroes and whites. On a similar co-operative basis Rosenwald brought about the building of more than five thousand Negro schools, shops, and homes for teachers in fifteen states, himself giving $4,000,000, or 15 per cent. He gave to Negro centers for higher education in Washington, Atlanta, Nashville, and New Orleans. Greatly distressed by the race riots in Chicago, he began to develop large-scale housing for Negroes with the Michigan Boulevard Garden Apartments.

Like Rabbi Hirsch, Rosenwald was anti-Zionist, but he helped those in need in the Near East and elsewhere, had a share in founding a publishing house in Tel-Aviv, and interested himself in a Palestinian agricultural experimental station. In 1914 he opposed a special Jewish organization for war relief, fearing that if it were set up, other agencies would refuse to help Jews, but by 1917 he was ready to give $1,000,000. Opposed to Communism, he also opposed those who sought to set up counterrevolutionary movements in Russia, and he was eager to co-operate with the Soviets in Jewish war relief as far as they would go. His gifts to German war widows and orphans after World War I and his encouragement of cultural relations between Germany and the United States earned him the personal thanks of President von Hindenburg.

In Chicago, Rosenwald got the YMCA Hotel started with a gift of $50,000. He gave $3,000,000 toward the Museum of Science and Industry, having desired such an institution for Chicago ever since 1911, when his son had been captivated by a similar museum in Munich. On his fiftieth birthday (1912), he announced public gifts of $687,500, including $250,000 to the University of Chicago, of which he was a trustee, inappropriately, he felt, since he had not finished high school. In 1916 he stimulated the establishment of a modern medical school by offering $500,-000 more. All in all he gave the university some four and a half millions.

In 1908, Illinois passed the first anti-pandering law in American history, and Rosenwald joined with Henry P. Crowell of Quaker Oats and the *Tribune* to put up the money for a fight on white slavery. In 1910 he was appointed to the Vice Commission. He was interested in the Franks case in 1914; later he contributed toward the Sacco and Vanzetti defense fund; he also helped to print the records of both the Sacco-Vanzetti case and the Mooney-Billings case. In local politics he opposed Thompson and supported Merriam and Dever. He helped subsidize *Harper's Weekly* when Norman Hapgood was editing it and *The United States Daily* when it was established by David Lawrence.

But Rosenwald's most spectacular giving was done within the Sears, Roebuck organization itself. When the firm had a serious financial crisis after World War I, he averted disaster by what amounted to guaranteeing the accounts of small stockholders; this involved a gift of about $5,000,000 and a loan of $4,000,000 more. But this was nothing compared to what he did in 1929, when he saved hundreds of persons from bankruptcy and spent $100,000,000 to guarantee the stock market accounts of all Sears, Roebuck employees who required such aid.

In 1917, Rosenwald went to France as Secretary of War Baker's representative. Meeting and lunching with him there, the Chicago newspaperman Howard Vincent O'Brien found him "crude, unpolished, naïve, but genuine and likeable and worthy of respect." The unfavorable aspects of this judgment are somewhat surprising, though there is no doubt that Rosenwald had his limitations of insight. A great reader of newspapers because they dealt with people, he was indifferent to the whole world of artistic values. Gloriously generous with millions, he was inclined to be penurious with pennies. He never favored higher salaries than the market rate, though he encouraged his employees to purchase stock and introduced profit-sharing and health and recreational benefits. When he testified in the investigation which followed the Vice Commission report, he could see no connection between a girl's moral downfall and the wages she received (the average wage for women at Sears' was then $9.12 a week).

Not even Jane Addams could teach him sound peace principles, and in 1916 he was beating the drums for universal military training. Yet when Jane Addams herself was under fire as the result of wartime hatreds, he stood by her loyally and helped organize the great testimonial dinner at the Merchandise Mart. He once took Grace Abbott in his car to a strike meeting where she was to speak, saying that he probably would not agree with a word she said but that he did not wish her to take cold on the way. He did not try to control the thinking of those who worked for him, nor did he believe that his own success was due wholly to his own ability. But though he was conservative in his social and political views, he could break ground when it needed to be broken. It took courage to finance a survey to uncover and treat venereal disease among Southern Negroes and elsewhere, and he advocated health insurance and group hospital contracts when the American Medical Association was still under the impression that they were "communistic."

Julius Rosenwald's career as a giver of mighty gifts finally taught him that it is easier to earn one million dollars than to dispose of it wisely. In 1917 he formed the Julius Rosenwald Fund, but he opposed tying up gifts in perpetuity and persuaded other foundations to modify their rules in this regard. He was a great Jew in a Gentile world; through him the noble universalism of Israel's greatest prophets expressed itself through a modern man of business.

IV

Perhaps Lorado Taft (1860–1936) impresses himself upon the consciousness of the art-minded visitor to Chicago beyond any other artist. If ever heavenly beauty shone through bronze, it illuminates the lovely forms and faces of *The Fountain of the Great Lakes*, just south of the Art Institute; and *The Solitude of the Soul*, which is inside, is, in its way, quite as moving. Out at the University of Chicago, the immense *Fountain of Time* dominates the west end of the Midway Plaisance.

Lorado Taft was born at Elmwood, in central Illinois. His father, Don Carlos Taft, was the son of a New Hampshire farmer, a clergyman, a college professor, and a "character." He taught geology at the University of Illinois, from which his son received both a bachelor's and a master's degree, but he taught so much else along with it that it was said of him that he occupied not a chair but a bench.

The boy found direction for his life at fourteen when he witnessed the unpacking of a shipment of plaster casts from Europe for the university's art museum. Sent to Paris to study sculpture, he responded generously to the French temperament and the artist's way of life but never modified his strict moral principles nor concealed his religious beliefs. In 1886, fortified by a commission for a statue of the Indiana statesman Schuyler Colfax, he returned to America. To keep alive he made plaster models for iron fireplace screens and modeled a butter woman for a fair. Asked if he ever prayed for success, he replied, "Oh, no, the other fellow might need it more than I." He became associated with Henry B. Fuller, Hamlin Garland, and Charles Francis Browne; both of the latter became his brothers-in-law. He taught at the Art Institute and began the career as public lecturer which lasted the rest of his life. He gave yearly series at the University of Chicago, but he also appeared in every state in the Union except Florida, which circumstance awakened him to a mused wondering "how they ever got along without me in Florida." At Evanston in 1891 he first gave the "Clay Talk" which involved modeling a lump of clay into various shapes. This became his most popular lecture and was given some fifteen hundred times.

Taft married in 1895 and settled in the Hyde Park district. At first he had a studio downtown in the Fine Arts Building, but in 1906 he moved his atelier to Hyde Park. Both here and at Eagle's Nest Camp in northern Indiana he gathered about him a company of young artists, many of whom had been attracted through his lectures. His birthdays were always gala affairs, celebrated with costume balls, banquets, or plays. One memorable event was a production of Maeterlinck's *The Blind*. Other productions included

A Midsummer Night's Dream, As You Like It, some Gilbert and Sullivan, and original works by members of the group.

The Fountain of Time was suggested by the words of Austin Dobson which are engraved upon it:

> Time goes, you say? Ah no,
> Alas, time stays. We go.

"The words brought before me a picture which fancy speedily transformed into a colossal work of sculpture. I saw the mighty crag-like figure of Time, mantled like one of Sargent's prophets, leaning upon his staff, his chin upon his hand, and watching with cynical, inscrutable gaze the endless march of humanity—a majestic relief of marble as I saw it, swinging in a wide circle around the form of the lone sentinel and made up of the shapes of hurrying men and women and children in endless procession, ever impelled by the winds of destiny in the inexorable lock-step of the ages. Theirs is the 'fateful forward movement' which has not ceased since time began. But in that crowded concourse how few detach themselves from the greyness of the dusty caravan, how few there are who even lift their heads. Here an overtaxed body falls—and a place is vacant for a moment; there a strong man turns to the silent, shrouded reviewer and with lifted arms utters the cry of the old-time gladiators: 'Hail Caesar, we who go to our death salute thee'—and presses forward."

The Fountain of Time was composed not of marble but of concrete mixed with crushed quartz rock, and concrete was used also for the heroic statue of Black Hawk which towers over the Rock River, near Oregon, Illinois. This statue involved a real engineering problem, including the building of a framework of timbers and steel rods covered with burlap and the employment of twenty-eight men to work in unbroken shifts day and night through the ten days which the pouring of the concrete required.

Lorado Taft would seem to have enjoyed a rich and happy life, yet no one better illustrates the truth of Browning's view that no true artist ever stops working until he reaches his point of failure. Impressive as *The Fountain of Time* is, in Taft's mind it was only one item in a comprehensive plan for the whole Midway Plaisance. The depression was to be flooded and spanned by three bridges, representing Religion, Science, and Art. *The Fountain of Time* at the west end was to be balanced by *The Fountain of Creation* in the east; at half-block intervals between were to stand statues of the world's great idealists. Much of this material was sketched and modeled, and some of the figures for *The Fountain of Creation* reached ten feet in plaster and even in Indiana limestone.

More ambitious still was the "Dream Museum," which, alas, was destined to remain wholly a dream. "My project contemplates an arrangement like a magnificent cathedral with many aisles, each one of which presents the masterpieces of a particular nation or race. These aisles would be crossed by transepts marking significant periods in the history of art. To trace the evolution of a national art, you would follow the aisle from east to west; to study the art of a particular century you would follow one of these transepts across the pageants of ten different countries. Thus you would find a cross section of the civilized world in the fifth century B. C.; again in the next century when Alexander led his triumphant hosts into the forgotten east; next, perhaps, the period of the so-called Roman Peace, about A. D. I (the birth of Christ); the reign of Charlemagne; the age of the Crusades; the cathedral builders; and the early and late Renaissance."

This might have been realized if Taft had succeeded in getting hold of the Fine Arts Building in Jackson Park. He pioneered in the movement to save this masterpiece, and in a way he was successful, but when Julius Rosenwald entered the picture, it became not an art museum but the Museum of Science and Industry, which was splendid in its way but not what Taft had intended. No wonder that he said, "I have fallen short of almost everything I have undertaken, but what a good time I have had in failing!" But like Browning himself, he knew and accepted this as the human condition, and his emphasis fell on the last half of the statement, not the first.

v

When I was a child, Ella Flagg Young was superintendent of the Chicago schools, and the first high school I attended—Harrison, the most beautiful high school building I have ever seen—was built during her administration. Children are not generally much concerned about the superintendent, but Mrs. Young was a controversial figure, partly because she held a position which, in those days, many people considered unsuited to a woman, partly because of her progressive policies, and partly because, lacking the wisdom of the serpent, she refused to build up a "machine" in the system and thus raised up many "interests" against her, all the way from textbooks to real estate.

I saw her only once, when I was in the eighth grade at the Plamondon School. She opened the door of our room one day while we were having our history lesson (we had been warned of her visitation) and slipped in, one of the littlest

99

women I had ever seen, with her hair combed back severely from her forehead but looking much less formidable than her pictures, walked to the back of the room, and returned to the door, when our principal, W. W. Reed, who taught eighth grade history, gestured the offer of a seat to her, which she silently declined in a deprecatory but very decided manner, and went out. She cannot have been in the room more than two minutes. I wonder what she would have said if she had been told that one of the children in that room would remember those two minutes across a lifetime and half a century later put her in a book!

Ella Flagg (her marriage, early in life, to one William Young, was a very brief one, terminated by his death) was born in Buffalo on January 15, 1845. Both her parents were of Scottish descent. Her father, though a mechanic, was a reading man who rebelled against the old Presbyterian rigidity, and in Chicago, to which the family removed when his daughter was thirteen, became a follower of David Swing. She passed her teacher's examination in 1860, when she was still too young to be given a certificate.

Her services to the Chicago public schools were well summed up in the resolution which the School Board passed on May 24, 1916:

"Mrs. Young retired from the office of superintendent of schools January 1, 1916. Her withdrawal from the system terminated a period of service which started in the year 1862, when she began as a grade teacher. In one year she was a head assistant. Two years later she became the first principal of the school of practice upon its creation as a part of the Chicago Normal School. At the end of six years she was given charge of the high-school class which developed into the South Division High School. After three years she returned to the Normal school as professor of mathematics, for two years. She then became principal of the Scammon School, which was followed by her principalship of the Skinner School.

"In 1887 she was made a district superintendent, which position she held until 1889, when she left the service and became, first, an associate professorial lecturer, and later, upon earning her doctor's degree, a full professor in the department of education at the University of Chicago. In 1905 she re-entered the school system as principal of the Chicago Normal School, which position she held until the year 1909, when she was elected superintendent of the public schools of this city.

"Mrs. Young was a member of the state board of education of Illinois for twenty-five years. She was elected president of the State Teachers' Association of Illinois in December, 1909, and in the year 1910 she was elected president of the National Education Association."

But it had not all been as peaceful as that sounds. Mrs. Young had tried to resign as superintendent in July 1913, but the Board had refused to accept her resignation and promised to support her policies. At one time a mass meeting of Chicago citizens jammed the Auditorium to demand her retention. As long as Carter Harrison was in office, she had support from the mayor's office, but when Thompson came in, he determined to get rid of her and finally made things so difficult as virtually to force her resignation.

At the University of Chicago, Mrs. Young was the special protégée of John Dewey, who testified that he had known only one other person "who so consistently reflected upon her experiences, digested them, turned them into significance or meanings for future use" and that he himself had often failed to see "the meaning or force of some favorite conception of my own till Mrs. Young had given it back to me."

A dedicated teacher, Mrs. Young had no patience with lazy or dishonest people, but she respected the sacredness of personality as few educators have ever respected it. Educational jargon concerning "the pedagogical child" was anathema to her; for her there was only *this* child, to be developed along the lines of his own endowment, and it was the teacher's business to find the way that was right for him. She would not permit supervising teachers to over-direct the cadets who worked under them and had only contempt for those of her subordinates who regarded faculty meetings as occasions for rubber-stamping policies which she had predetermined. Some members of the faculty at Chicago Normal wanted her to give them her "philosophy of education," but she refused. "All that people desire me to do," she said, "is to give them some stock phrases which they can use on all occasions instead of doing their own thinking."

From her father Mrs. Young inherited an interest in mathematics, and during her early years she tended to favor mathematics over other subjects because of its conciseness and susceptibility to demonstration. Later she changed her mind about this. Human nature was more interesting than numbers, and the things which were most important could not be demonstrated. As time passed, indeed, she tended to sit more lightly on all the traditional disciplines, and her interest in technical education gave her enemies a chance to say that she was turning Chicago into a city of trade schools. She became interested in nature study and encouraged instruction in drawing and in manual training. At one time she even insisted that not girls only but even boys must learn how to sew, for who knew when life might bring them to a pass where they might need to sew on their own buttons? How I hated her for these things, and how she made me suffer in the woodworking shop! I should have hated her even more for her interest in physical education if I had known about it, but she didn't "get" me on that score, for our school had no gymnasium! Actually, as I now realize, she had not lowered her educational ideals; she simply knew that if you are going to educate a child, you must begin where he lives. Early in her career she was assigned to the "cowboy class" in the Foster School. She conquered the boys by being simultaneously and immovably firm and fair, and late one afternoon the "cowboy" who had troubled her most came in to remonstrate with her over her habit of staying in her room to correct papers until nightfall. In such a neighborhood, he told her, it was not safe for her to go home alone after dark. That was when she knew that she had won.

I suspect Mrs. Young's job in Chicago would have been much easier if all the children under her had had my educational interests (though what she would have done about my inability to learn the multiplication table I have no idea), but they had not, and she recognized it frankly, realizing too that these boys and girls still must be prepared for life and for decent, useful citizenship. She tried to teach us that working with your hands is as respectable as working with your head, and that pride taken in the work of one's hands is a legitimate pride. It is for lack of such common sense as this that our colleges are crowded today with people who ought never to have been sent there, while our workingmen imperil our standing among the nations by centering their attention not upon their work but on the time clock and the "coffee break." Ventilation, heating, and lighting are not education, but the lack of them can vitiate the efforts of the best teacher, and Mrs. Young did not find them unworthy of her attention. Bathing is not education either, but this did not keep her from installing the first school bath in Chicago in a district that needed it. She provided special courses for the handicapped, and she pioneered in the teaching of sex hygiene.

She consulted teachers about the curriculum, advanced them on merit, and abolished the system of secret marking which had been used before her. Her appointments were on a merit basis, without regard to her personal attitude toward the appointee or the appointee's attitude toward her. She championed the right of teachers to organize on the ground that they were citizens and that no right which any citizen possessed could be denied them. Her office was open at any hour to any Chicagoan who chose to visit her; until near the end of her superintendency she did not even have a secretary.

Though Mrs. Young died on October 26, 1918, her portrait still hangs in the Teachers Room at the Chicago Public Library. It is unusual for a superintendent to be remembered so long and so well. This is not only because of her ability, able as she was. Nor is it basically a question of whether she was right in all her policies. She was an incorruptible human being who lived for the single purpose of developing Chicago's children into the best and wisest human beings it was possible for them to be.

5

—————— *The Greatest Chicagoan of All* ——————

In this chapter title I do use the superlative—and mean it. From the autumn of 1889, when she and Ellen Gates Starr opened the doors of Hull-House, just off Halsted Street, in a slum neighborhood on the near West Side which had become a melting pot for many nations, until her death in May, 1935, Jane Addams was prominently identified with virtually every social and international movement looking toward the remaking of the sordid unrealities of contemporary living into something approximating the symmetrical beauty of an ordered righteousness.

Jane Addams did not begin the settlement-house movement, even in Chicago. There was the Eli Bates Settlement as early as 1876. Neither did she monopolize it, for among her contemporaries there were, to mention no more, Graham Taylor of the Chicago Commons and the University of Chicago's Mary McDowell, "the Angel of the Stockyards," who lived to transform that neighborhood of horror into a place fit for human beings to live in. Yet it seems to me incontestable that Jane Addams was Chicago's first citizen, and if she was not also the greatest woman who ever lived in this country, then I do not know who was.

She touched life in so many different ways that it is puzzling to know how best to approach her. I am going to try approaching her in what I know must seem to many the unlikeliest way possible—as an artist. Born in Cedarville, Illinois, in 1860, she was herself, inevitably, moved by the beauties of nature long before she had made any vital contact with the beauty that is art. Years later, when she first came to know city children, their inaccessibility to beauty was one of the things for which she pitied them, but she was even more impressed by the pitiful contrast between the free-ranging country games in which she had shared and the constant interruptions with which their play was forced to contend, "the most elaborate 'plan or chart' or 'fragment from their dream of human life'" being "sure to be rudely destroyed by the passing traffic." In the settlement they used art from the beginning for all there was in it, and the very first building they erected at Hull-House was an art gallery.

As the years went by, Jane Addams savored art in other aspects than as a vehicle of self-expression. Sometimes she thought of it as an attempt "to satisfy, outside of life, those cravings which life leaves unsatisfied." She felt the need of vision as the artist feels it, was time and again under the necessity of renewing her life-perceptions; she experienced too the value of the sudden, intuitive illumination that the artist so often knows. Her own brilliant study of "The Devil Baby at Hull-House," that fascinating piece of contemporary folklore, is a striking revelation of her own ability to probe experience, to interpret it, to extract the last bit of significance from it, as only the sympathetic imagination of the artist can.

At the same time she came early to the conclusion that art was not enough. Like Bernard Shaw, she was drawn powerfully in two directions at once, having at the same time a profound sensitiveness to beauty and a deep, underlying conscientiousness which insisted that there was something guilty in the appreciation of beauty for its own sake and without reference to the contribution it could make to the amelioration of the sad state of mankind. Only in such artists as Albrecht Dürer could the two elements seem to fuse, "taking his wonderful pictures, however, in the most unorthodox manner, merely as human documents. I was chiefly appealed to by his unwillingness to lend himself to a smooth and cultivated view of life, by his determination to record its frustrations and even the hideous forms which darken the day for our human imagination and to ignore no human complications."

As she grew older, life claimed her more and art less. Like Browning, like Stevenson, like Willa Cather, she found life itself more interesting than any re-creation of it could be. "While I receive valuable suggestions from classical literature, when I really want to learn about life, I must depend upon my neighbors." It was as if the purely aesthetic impulse as generally defined was too individualistic, too self-centered to serve her needs.

Yet if she often thought of art in terms of social service, then it is also true that she often thought of social service in terms of art. "The chief characteristic of art lies in freeing the individual from a sense of separation and isolation in his emotional experience, and has usually been accomplished through painting, writing, and singing; but this does not make it in the least impossible that it is now being tried, self-consciously and most bunglingly, we will admit, in terms of life itself." And perhaps it was while remembering the old Gothic cathedrals and other community enterprises of days gone by that she could declare further: "The genius for goodness has in the past largely expressed itself through individuals and groups, but it may be that we are approaching a period which shall give it collective expression, and shall unite into one all those private and parochial efforts."

II

She had this "genius for goodness." She inherited a terrible thirst for righteousness from her Puritan forebears. Yet the prime motive that led to the foundation of Hull-House seems to have been the old, simple, unadulterated impulse of human pity. Even as a child she was troubled by the inequalities of life. One day she asked her father why the poor people of Cedarville lived "in such horrid little houses so close together," and when he replied that their circumstances did not permit them to live otherwise, she declared firmly that when she grew up she would live in a large house, "but it would not be built among the other large houses, but right in the midst of horrid little houses like these." But her real baptism of fire came much later in London, where the misery and squalor of an East London slum so smote her that nothing else in Europe seemed of any consequence in comparison.

But it is one thing to be struck with a sense of pity. It is quite another to give your life to correcting, even a little, the circumstances of which you complain. Such a way of life, in the first place, means labor. In the early days this was often physical labor of the hardest and most uninteresting kind. It never ceased to mean incessant, patient ministry to the small needs of hosts of insignificant and in many cases ungrateful people. It also meant continually coming into conflict with all the predatory interests of the city, to say nothing of the even more trying conflict with those who should be on your side yet for some reason or other utterly fail to understand what you are doing. Sometimes it meant rendering dangerous emergency service, as when, during a smallpox epidemic, Hull-House served as a head-quarters for the smallpox inspectors. And for a woman like Jane Addams, never physically strong, often prostrated by critical illness, it meant too a never ceasing nervous strain, of which one catches a faint glimpse in her remark, "In spite of poignant experiences, or, perhaps, because of them, the memory of the first years at Hull-House is more or less blurred with fatigue."

But there is another thing that is more precious than labor and harder to come by, and this is charity, under-standing. Jane Addams saw the worst sights of her genera-tion; she was familiar with every phase of the sacrifice of human values that is exacted when a great city places a purely commercial valuation upon the impulses of youth. These things left their mark upon her. Francis Hackett spoke of her face "swept so often by shadows as far hills are swept by a shadow when a cloud moves across them." Yet she insisted uncompromisingly on "the very energy of existence, the craving for enjoyment, the pushing of vital forces, the very right of every citizen to be what he is with-out pretence or assumption of virtue." Understandingly—and generously—she spoke of "humbler people, who sin often through weakness and passion but seldom through hardness of heart." And as far as the social worker at least was concerned, she believed that sympathy must never be "alienated by wrongdoing," for true love and patience "ministers to need irrespective of worth." Or, as she put it more specifically, the work of the settlement is "grounded in a philosophy whose foundation is on the solidarity of the human race, a philosophy which will not waver when the race happens to be represented by a drunken woman or an idiot boy."

III

My old friend William E. Barton, biographer of Lincoln, pastor of the First Congregational Church of Oak Park during my high school days, and so long a power in the religious life of the Chicago area, used to enjoy telling how, one day, as he sat down with Jane Addams and others at the first meeting of a new civic committee, she looked about at the faces of her tablemates and remarked, "Well, I see it's the same old bunch. What's your name today?" And she herself has recorded her amusement when the elevator boy in a Loop building asked her, as he took her up to a noonday conference, "What are you lunching with today? Is it garbage or the social evil?" They were all the same to her; once she was the garbage inspector for her ward. In 1899, Chicago established the first juvenile court in America; Hull-House played an important part in setting it up, as it did in the passage of the child labor law as far back as 1893 and a thousand other things besides.

"Miss Addams," wrote Ralph Fletcher Seymour, "seemed to be always a little hurried, a little sad, a little restrained and detached. Her responsibilities were great and she had a lot of helpers who tried to shield her from meeting everybody." So she must have impressed the casual observer, but she was never shielded from her neighbors. If there was a baby to deliver and no midwife at hand, she could do it. If a frightened child was dying, she could take him in her arms and allay his fears, and if you needed somebody to bathe a baby or comb a sick woman's hair, she was ready for that too. But possibly you only wanted a friend to drop in for a cup of coffee and sit down, perhaps on the floor, for a chat, and it is remarkable that Jane Addams was never too busy for that either. She used to assure people that the reason she lived in an industrial neighborhood was that she found it more interesting than any other part of the city, and she made the Hull-House dinner hour as much a thing of grace and beauty as it could have been on the lake front of the North Shore. One night she was in Louise de Koven Bowen's box at the opera. When the lights went on, Mrs. Bowen noticed that she had her feet tucked away suspiciously under her skirts. She had taken off her shoes because her feet hurt, and when Mrs. Bowen told her that she must put them on because visitors were expected during the intermission, her reply admitted of no discussion. "I won't," she said, and she didn't.

She disliked the phrase "sociological laboratory" in its application to the settlement as much as Ella Flagg Young disliked hearing about "the pedagogical child." She was hurt when one of her associates spoke of the "important people" who were lost on the *Titanic*. So she escaped all the pitfalls and dangers of the reforming temperament as commonly conceived. "It is always easy for those in pursuit of ends which they consider of overwhelming importance to become themselves thin and impoverished in spirit and temper, to gradually develop a dark mistaken eagerness alternating with fatigue, which supersedes 'the great and gracious ways' so much more congruous with worthy aims."

All this, I suppose, is simply another way of saying that in Jane Addams we had an almost abnormal development of the hunger for fellowship; she had an almost mystical sense of the unity of all mankind. Like Tolstoy, she found the essence of immorality in making an exception of oneself; the quicksands of self-righteousness wait to engulf those who think themselves unlike their brethren. It was this passion for fellowship which made her position during World War I—a comparative isolation in which a self-conscious egotist might have rejoiced—such exquisite torture for her. "The force of the majority was so overwhelming that it seemed not only impossible to hold one's own against it, but at moments absolutely unnatural, and one secretly yearned to participate in the 'folly of all mankind.'"

But it would be a serious understatement to say merely that Jane Addams was free from all sense of superiority toward those to whom she ministered; in many cases she also felt a genuine reverence for them. They learned from her but she also learned from them. How wonderfully illuminating is a passage in her *Newer Ideals of Peace*. "The eighteenth century humanitarian," she begins, "hotly insisted upon the 'rights of man,' but he loved the people without really knowing them, which is by no means an impossible achievement. 'The love of those whom a man does not know is quite as elemental a sentiment as the love of those whom a man does know,' but with this difference . . . ." With this difference, you or I might have continued, that those whom we do not know never have an opportunity to try our patience, to disillusion us. But Jane Addams goes on: "with this difference, that he shuts himself away from the opportunity of being caught and carried forward in the stream of their hopes and aspirations, a bigger and warmer current than he dreams of."

The immigrants brought many skills to Hull-House, much beauty and interest, as all who have visited the labor museum there know, but their best contributions were nonmaterial. Upon the residents they had a profoundly liberalizing effect; in Jane Addams personally they contributed to the development of a charity and tolerance as wide as the world, to that deeper comprehension of life that always comes with a genuine appreciation of other ways and other viewpoints. Where did Jane Addams learn her wisdom but in the slums? Who spread "the treasure of the humble" before her? She did not develop her "newer ideals of peace" in the study. In college she never got beyond *Heroes and Hero-Worship*. But in the settlement she perceived that great changes do not come about through individual thinkers but flow along half-formulated, half-realized currents of thought and feeling in the heart of a people.

But if Jane Addams had charity toward publicans and sinners, she met another test also: she had good will toward the scribes and the Pharisees. The local political background of her later autobiographical narrative, *The Second Twenty Years at Hull-House*, is supplied by perhaps the most openly and flagrantly corrupt political machine in the history of American politics. Jane Addams kept her pen free from bitterness and disillusionment, never permitted herself the luxury of even a flurry of righteous indignation. Not even when she touches the abysmal stupidities of the D.A.R. blacklist does her humor desert her. In 1900 she was made an honorary member of the D.A.R. "I supposed at the time that it had been for life, but it was apparently only for good behavior."

Such charity might be easy for a sentimentalist, but Jane Addams was never that. Has any piece of writing ever thrown the monstrous ignorance and instability of Henry Ford into more glaring relief than her cool, objective analysis of the Peace Ship adventure? And did any writer ever achieve a more penetrating analysis of the limitations or the curious contradictions in Woodrow Wilson? "It seemed to us at moments as if the President were imprisoned in his own spacious intellectuality, and had forgotten the overwhelming value of the deed." She wondered: "What was this curious break between speech and deed, how could he expect to know the doctrine if he refused to do the will?" And when, on avowedly idealistic grounds, the President decided to take America into the war, she asked herself "whether any man had the right to rate his moral leadership so high that he could consider the sacrifice of the lives of thousands of his young countrymen a necessity?"

IV

None of her gifts of heart could ever have served Jane Addams as they did without the fine, penetrating intelligence controlling them or the sturdy common sense behind them. Her work brought her into almost daily contact with what one of her friends, Theodore Roosevelt, called the "lunatic fringe" of the reforming movement, but she managed, quite consistently, to keep herself free of their numerous vagaries. She could admire grand gestures when others made them; hers was the quieter, more difficult task of carrying on the work of public education, and steadily developing a sense of public obligation clear down the weary years.

With this in mind she cherished an eclectic ideal, consistently refused to commit Hull-House to any definite propaganda program. As she saw it, the settlement house was a clearinghouse for every kind of propaganda, but it must not identify itself with any particular kind. Once a labor leader told her that she would change her tune when she began to be subsidized by millionaires, and she immediately replied that she intended neither to be subsidized by millionaires nor bullied by workingmen. Thus Socialists and other groups were often impatient with her, and she with them because she saw them leaving the realm of experience to take refuge in theory. Herself she had no passion for rash generalizations. When the controversy over "tainted money" was at its height, Hull-House kept itself free from all suspicion of evil by refusing to partake of such funds, yet when Jane Addams was asked to write or speak on the subject, she always declined, for she "never felt clear enough on the general principle involved." Nothing could have been more characteristic of her than the statement she made at the testimonial banquet given in her honor in Chicago in January, 1927: "I am very grateful for the affection and interest you have brought here this evening; yet in a way humiliated by what you say I am, for I know myself to be a very simple person, not at all sure I am right, and most of the time not right, though wanting to be; which I am sure we all know of ourselves."

In the best sense of a much abused word, she was, then, an opportunist; she was for the "best possible." Though she had many disappointments, she was saved from despair by the fact that she had never expected too much. Neither did she ever lose her ability to view the situation from the other fellow's point of view. Take liquor, for example. No one opposed liquor more intelligently, for nobody understood the essential lawlessness of the liquor interests better, or was more poignantly aware of the intimate connection between liquor and poverty, prostitution, and crime. "But if alcohol was associated intensively with these gross evils, it was also associated with homely and wholesome things," with sociability and fellowship and camaraderie. Take the slum boys and their "gangs." She knew the gangs for the menace that they were, saw their existence as at once a challenge and a rebuke to a city that had failed to make any provision for the social needs of youth. And yet "nothing is more for-

lorn than the boy who has no gang at whose fire of friend-
ship he may warm himself." Like Samuel McChord Croth-
ers, she knew that "it is the province of mercy to treat each
case as, in a sense, an exception." Like Cowper, she knew
that those who are to do us good must do it in our way and
not in theirs.

Probably Jane Addams' scientific bent and her early scientific training had something to do with her open-mindedness. Her first ambition was to be a physician. Perhaps her
realism nowhere showed up more attractively than in her
attitude toward sex. Nowadays, of course, it requires no
courage to speak of sex; indeed it requires courage not to
speak of it. But in the days when Jane Addams began to
urge the teaching of sex hygiene in the public schools, the
situation was very different. Everything that is valid in
Freud she knew long before what E. E. Stoll used to call
"the bad news out of Vienna" began to blow our way, and
it is to the austere inspiration of our legion of lost youth
that we owe the most beautiful book she ever wrote, *The
Spirit of Youth and the City Streets.*

v

Hitherto I have spoken of Jane Addams' salient qualities
in a rather general way, choosing illustrations of each from
varied phases of her manifold activities. There are some
lines of interest, however, in which all her qualities seem
to be illustrated, drawn together as it were, concentrated
upon a single problem.

First of all, let us return to this matter of wayward youth.
How wise Jane Addams was here and how charitable! "It
may relieve the mind to break forth in moments of irritation
against 'the folly of the coming generation,' but whoso
pauses on his plodding way to call even his youngest and

rashest brother a fool, ruins thereby the joy of his journey, —for youth is so vivid an element in life that unless it is cherished, all the rest is spoiled." She never thought of juvenile crime as evidence of innate degeneration; in many cases children go astray merely because they are suffering from an overstimulated imagination. While as for sexual delinquencies, we have only ourselves to blame, for the modern city, as we have built it, incessantly stimulates the senses of youth on every hand yet never provides any legitimate gratification for them. "Above all we cannot hope that they will understand the emotional force which seizes them and which, when it does not find the traditional line of domesticity, serves as a cancer in the very tissue of society and as a disrupter of the securest social bonds."

Then there was the problem of the theater. In the old days the Hull-House neighborhood was honeycombed with cheap, popular melodrama theaters. To Jane Addams it seemed a pity that "the only art which is continually before the eyes of 'the temperamental youth' " should be "a debased form of dramatic art and a vulgar type of music," but she did not therefore lose her ability to view "the house of dreams" through her neighbors' eyes. "If we agree with a recent definition of Art as that which causes the spectator to lose his sense of isolation, there is no doubt that the popular theater, with all its faults, more nearly fills this function or art for the multitude of working people than all the 'free galleries' and picture exhibits combined."

Later on the motion picture came along, and from the beginning Jane Addams was fully awake to both its possibilities and its dangers. In 1907 she presented a resolution at the City Club advocating regulation, not suppression, of the five-cent theaters. For a time Hull-House operated a picture theater of its own, attempting through clean surroundings and carefully chosen subjects to avoid the objectionable features found in other theaters of the period. The problems raised by the motion picture are not solved, and as long as she lived, Jane Addams was familiar with them all, but she never forgot that "the function of release in neighborhoods such as ours, is marvelously performed by the movies."

In its more serious aspects the drama was always a part of the Hull-House program, and one remembers the historic performance of *Justice* which so impressed Theodore Roosevelt long before the name of John Galsworthy was widely or generally familiar in the United States. In such a production the drama itself becomes a source of refreshment and enlightenment, an interpretation of life. "One never ceases to marvel at the power of even a mimic stage to afford to the young a magic space in which life may be lived in efflorescence, where manners may be courtly and elaborate without exciting ridicule, where the sequence of events is impressive and comprehensible." But here again art is not enough, for it is in God's world, not in some fresh creation of our own, that our real business lies. "To insist that young people shall forecast their rose-colored future only in a house of dreams, is to deprive the real world of the warmth and reassurance which it so sorely needs and to which it is justly entitled."

As the third and last expression of Jane Addams' character, we may glance at her work for peace. There was nothing doctrinaire, nothing namby-pamby about her pacifism. Nonresistance she thought a misleading term. "It suggests passivity, the goody-goody attitude of ineffectiveness." Nor did she unreservedly follow Tolstoy, much as she admired him. Tolstoy's appeal is dogmatic, boils down to the command to cease to do evil. "And when this same line of appeal is presented by less gifted men, it often results in mere sentimentality, totally unenforced by a call to righteousness."

Jane Addams was not slandered in 1917–18 as John Peter Altgeld had been slandered in another connection, but many of the things that were said about her were quite bad enough. Nobody was more moved by the heroism of the war than she, nobody more ready to give due meed of praise to devotion wherever it was found. And nobody was more anxious to help; nobody suffered more keenly from being left out. She had never believed with Ibsen that the strongest man was the man who stood alone. All her emphasis had been social; her whole influence had been used to bring Americans together to work for the common good. Now at last they were united, united in a common cause as they had never before been united in her time, all their energies devoted to what millions of them honestly believed to be a holy crusade, believed in so ardently that they were willing to slay and be slain in its behalf. But that was just the trouble. Jane Addams had always been a creator, nurturing life, upbuilding it; she could not now turn suddenly about and begin to destroy it. As Francis Hackett acutely suggested, for her the war was a civil war. "She *knew* the combatants. She could not have made Hull House without knowing them." She tried to be reasonable in a world gone mad.

VI

There was no formal religious instruction at Hull-House, the residents themselves were men and women of all creeds and none, and during the early years the institution was often attacked in evangelical circles in Chicago as irreligious. Yet when John Burns visited Chicago, he spoke of Jane Addams as "the only saint America has produced," and her nephew James Weber Linn ends his biography of her with the words, "If Jane Addams were truly representative, we should now be living in the millennium."

If Micah's definition of religion is adequate, Jane Addams surely deserves to be called a saint, and it is clear that her own inspiration was broadly and humanly—though quite undogmatically—Christian. She grew up in a Christian atmosphere (though her father was not actually a member of any church), and during her childhood she went through all the mental disquiet that sensitive children so often had to suffer under the old evangelicalism. She worried about foreordination and the end of the world; she thought of hell; she faced the terrible finality of death. But already her rationalism was developing: she could not share the fear of her pious neighbors that the good village doctor who had died might not go to heaven because he had not been a "professing" Christian. At boarding school in Rockford much pressure was brought upon her to "profess" her own salvation, but the realism and scrupulous honesty which distinguished her later career had already claimed her. Her "experience" had not conformed to the prescribed pattern; she was too honest to pretend that it had; she remained therefore perforce among the unconverted. During these years too she gravitated toward Darwinism and toward positivism, and neither interest tended to bring her into harmony with a dogmatic orthodoxy as she understood it. It was indeed not until she had reached maturity and was almost ready to begin her life work that she finally received baptism and became a member of the Presbyterian church. "While I was not conscious of any emotional 'conversion,' I took upon myself the outward expressions of the religious life with all humility and sincerity. . . . I was conscious of no change from my childish acceptance of the teachings of the Gospels, but at this moment something persuasive within me made me long for an outward symbol of fellowship, some bond of peace, some blessed spot where unity of spirit might claim right of way over all differences." It is interesting to note that even when she did finally unite with a church, it was a sociological kind of religion that possessed her: she felt "an almost passionate devotion to the ideals of democracy, and when in all history," she asked, "had those ideals been so thrillingly expressed as when the faith of the fisherman and the slave had been boldly opposed to the accepted moral belief that the well-being of a privileged few might justly be built upon the ignorance and sacrifice of the many?"

It is true of course that if Jane Addams were a girl today, she would escape many phases of the spiritual struggle of her youth. Yet not, perhaps, all. I have been greatly interested to note her many unpremeditated expressions of her bewilderment in the face of the mystery of life. Thus she speaks of "the melodramatic coarseness of life, which Stevenson more gently described as 'the uncouth and outlandish strain in the web of the world,'" of those "mysterious and impersonal wrongs which are apparently inherent in the very nature of things," or "that shadow which already lurks only around the corner for most of us—a skepticism of life's value." Work—duty—service—even love—these things, it seems, are not, after all, quite enough. Perhaps we cannot love mercy and do justly except we also walk humbly with God, "which may mean to walk for many dreary miles beside the lowliest of his creatures, not even in that peace of mind which the company of the humble is popularly supposed to afford, but rather with the pangs and throes to which the poor human understanding is subjected whenever it attempts to comprehend the meaning of life."

Even in this note of mild and reverent skepticism, however, one cannot but find a corollary to the honesty, the open-mindedness, the sensitive receptivity that lay at the root of Jane Addams' finest achievements. The eclectic ideal has its limitations, but it has its advantages also, and if Jane Addams was not wholly scientist or artist or religionist, still she understood and somewhat employed advantageously all these three avenues of approach, and, for that very reason, her work as a whole was marked by none of the shortcomings too often consequent upon an exclusive reliance on any one of them. If America is ever to be saved, it will not be her atom bombs that will save her; it will be because she still has in her the stuff of such humanity as for her generation was embodied outstandingly in Jane Addams.

6

The Craft of Letters

"CHICAGO," wrote Evelyn F. Carlson in 1947, "publishes more trade catalogues and telephone directories than any other city in the world. It has the world's largest mail-order business; one of the mail-order houses alone prints one million catalogues yearly." Even if we take with a grain of salt H. L. Mencken's famous statements of the early twenties that Chicago was the literary center of America and that practically all American writers of consequence had been molded by her, it must still be granted that she has had her share of both literary production and literary consumption. Once distinguished as publishers and still prominent in the wholesale trade, A. C. McClurg and Company also operated a great bookstore in the days of my youth; during more recent times the town has benefited from the ministrations of one of the great men of the book trade, "Papa" Kroch, who began in a small shop in Monroe Street, where he would not stock books he considered worthless, however great the demand might be. Marshall Field's, too, have built up a vast book section, attracting public attention through book fairs, lectures, autographing parties, and special exhibits. Walter M. Hill kept a fine shop in Van Buren Street, and in the twenties it was always a pleasure to buy at the friendly little store which Fanny Butcher operated in Adams Street, near the Art Institute.

Yet, though Chicago has the leading geographical publishers in Rand, McNally and a very distinguished scholarly press at the University of Chicago, compared to Boston, or even Philadelphia, her book-publishing record as a whole is somewhat disappointing. When Chicago publishers do make a success, they are likely to move to New York, as Pascal Covici did or Pellegrini and Cudahy, and even *Esquire*, though in this case *Playboy* promptly stepped into the breach. Reilly and Lee have lived on the "Oz" books of L. Frank Baum and his successors, though the first, *The Wizard of Oz*, was originally published not by them but by George M. Hill; it was written in Chicago as well as published there and may well rank as the most successful book that ever came out of the town. Generally, however, one thinks of Chicago publishing in terms of such popularizing enterprises as the "Lakeside Library" of the seventies, the first ten-cent series of fiction reprints—imitated in the East by the "Seaside Library" and others; the Book Supply Company, which was organized to distribute the novels of Harold Bell Wright; *Who's Who in America*; the *Encyclopaedia Britannica*; a vast array of trade papers and religious papers, including the distinguished *Christian Century*; and the millions of copies of *Time*, *Life*, etc. which pour from R. R. Donnelley and Sons' Lakeside Press, though their editorial offices are in New York. Once, however, just after the World's Columbian Exposition, Melville Stone's son, Herbert S. Stone, who went down with the *Lusitania*, operated the extraordinary firm of Stone and Kimball, later Herbert S. Stone and Company, producers of beautiful trade editions of the works of many respected modern writers, both American and foreign (they were

Bernard Shaw's first American publishers) and of a delightful literary potpourri, *The Chap-Book*, though even here it is ironical that their greatest commercial success should have been the trashy *Story of Mary MacLane*. For a time, Way and Williams did the same kind of thing. The great typographers Fred and Bertha Goudy were associated with the publisher Ralph Fletcher Seymour; their press was in a basement apartment on the South Side, and here the first of their Village Press books were issued. The Caxton Club has been publishing fine limited editions for its members since 1895; a smaller, shorter-lived organization was the Dofobs Society ("Damned Old Fools Over Books").

II

Newspapers, of course, are another story, and newspaper life in Chicago has always been exciting and not infrequently rowdy. Schlogl's restaurant, a newspaperman's hangout, long carried a mysterious item on the menu "owls to order," and if one is to believe all that has been written of the Whitechapel Club, its members must have been criminal lunatics. From 1939, when Hearst discontinued his morning paper, the *Herald-Examiner*, and changed the name of his evening paper, the *American*, to the *Herald-American*, until 1941, when Marshall Field III was inspired by his devotion to F.D.R. to establish the *Sun* in opposition to the *Tribune*, Chicago had but one morning paper, and since 1956, when the *Tribune* bought the *Herald-American* and renamed it *Chicago's American*, there have been but two morning and two evening papers, one of each pair controlled by the Patterson-McCormick interests and the others by the Field interests. In 1947, Field purchased the *Times* tabloid, which he combined the next year with the *Sun* as the *Sun-Times*, and in 1959, Field Enterprises bought the *Daily News* from John Knight, who had controlled it since Frank Knox passed out of the picture in 1944.

It was not always so. In 1900 there were ten English dailies published in Chicago, and in the nineteenth century there were more than that. The foreign language press (German, Czech, Yiddish, etc.) has always been important, and now the Negroes have not only the *Daily Defender* but such magazines as *Ebony*, *Jet*, and the *Negro Digest*.

Of the living newspapers of Chicago, the *Tribune* is much the oldest, having been born in 1847 out of a literary paper known as *Gem of the Prairie*. By any strictly journalistic test—news coverage, editorial vigor, the vitality of its services, and the range and appeal of its features—it is one of the great ranking newspapers of the world, but it has rarely failed to serve as a storm center, and during the years of its bitter, consistent opposition to F.D.R.'s New Deal, one might almost have said that Chicagoans were divided not between men and women but rather between those who loved the *Tribune* and those who hated it. "Only —— Days Left to Save Your Country" was carried on the front page all through the Campaign of 1936, and when the President arrived to speak at the Chicago Stadium, the police actually feared that his partisans would attack *Tribune* and Hearst press cars. Before the first number of the *Sun* appeared, there had been a public meeting supporting the administration's foreign policy, from which it is said people emerged to buy *Tribunes* and burn them in the street, thus boosting the circulation figures even higher. Colonel McCormick could well afford to smile at such antics, and at the "Colonel McCosmic" cartoons in the *Daily News*, which testified to his importance in the eyes of his enemies, and if the *Sun* sold 900,000 copies its first day (though dropping thereafter to a figure between 300,000 and 360,000), everybody had to buy the *Tribune* too, since the extra-large banner head-line read "F.D.R.'S WAR PLAN!"—perhaps the greatest "scoop" since the printing of the Versailles Treaty in 1919.

It was interesting to remember that the *Tribune* had also been resisting war fever in 1914–17, when the Colonel's eccentric, socialistically inclined cousin, Joseph Medill Patterson, who lost fourteen million dollars of *Tribune* money on the magazine *Liberty* and afterwards made a smashing success of the New York *Daily News*, was in charge. It was Burton Rascoe's judgment that Patterson's *Notebook of a Neutral*, serialized in the *Tribune*, was "the only book of the hysterical period before we entered the war which calmly, clearly, logically and with facts strove to offset the effect of British propaganda in this country and the pro-Ally attempts of the wealthy classes of America to drag us into the war." Yet the dove of peace did not really roost in Patterson's cotes, for he admitted his sympathy with the ideas of Bernhardi and had no objection to our entering the war if we could make terms to our own advantage, looking forward to our own "inevitable" war with Japan and the establishment of a "protectorate" over Mexico. Mc-Cormick, on the other hand, despite some inconsistencies, gave the impression of a sincere devotion to peace abroad and liberty at home, and there were times when *Tribune* editorials during World War II almost reached the level of a representative spokesman of the Fellowship of Recon-ciliation or the Society of Friends. It was the fashion among McCormick's enemies to depict the publisher as a roaring lion going about seeking whom he might devour; as usual, any resemblances between legend and reality were purely coincidental. When the *Tribune*'s chief cartoonist, the great John T. McCutcheon, refused, during the early years of the New Deal, to attack F.D.R. on the domestic front because his own convictions were not in line with the policy of his paper (he had previously refused to attack prohibition), no pressure of any kind was brought to bear upon him, and it was not until after Roosevelt's "Quarantine" speech in Chicago, dedicating the Outer Drive Bridge, on December 5, 1937, almost in the presence of a large wharf sign "CHICAGO TRIBUNE UNDOMINATED," that the cartoonist, convinced that the President was now implacably set on war, went to his drawing board to conduct his own campaign against him.

The *Tribune-Sun* antagonism being what it was, it is amusing to recall that the money with which the Colonel's grandfather, Joseph Medill, builder of the *Tribune* and the dominating figure in its early history, bought majority stock control was borrowed from Marshall Field! In 1945 the *Tribune* finally lost its fight to deny the *Sun* AP service, and after McCormick's death, ten years later, it was a *Sun-Times* man who suggested that McCormick Place be named in his honor. Medill, too, had been a controversial figure, not without his idiosyncrasies. A strong temperance man, he helped found the Keeley cure and prescribed it for *Tribune* men who needed it. "One brute pounds another for the benefit of a gang of other brutes" was his description of a boxing match; as a matter of fact, he disliked the sports page in general. He also disapproved of stock-market news on the ground that it encouraged gambling. But he opposed the eight-hour day and was a bitter enemy of Altgeld and his kind, and he looked forward to clearing the British out of Canada. In 1875, with one eye on the communists, he even argued that "Judge Lynch is an American, by birth and character." In 1898, like Hearst, he was for war with Spain, opposing Marshall Field and other merchant princes of Chicago. But his son-in-law, Robert

Patterson, adhered firmly to the principle that news stories must be presented without bias, and in Pullman-strike days refused to obey the old man's edict that Debs must always be referred to as "Dictator Debs."

Nothing in *Tribune* history can match for sensationalism the old *Times* during the Wilbur F. Storey period. "Telegraph fully all news and when there is no news send rumors" —this was the standing order. "JERKED TO JESUS" above the report of a hanging was merely the most sensational of many alliterative headlines. Shows at McVicker's were damned, good or bad, for personal reasons, and the actress Lydia Thompson was quite justified when she tried to horsewhip Storey on the street for "BAWDS AT THE OPERA HOUSE! WHERE'S THE POLICE?" During the Civil War, Storey was the consistent opponent of Lincoln and champion of Vallandigham and the Copperheads; on June 3, 1863, General Burnside played into his hands by trying to suppress the paper in the interest of national security. Friends and foes of the *Times* joined to urge Lincoln to countermand the order, which he did two days later. But it was a real crisis while it lasted, with the antiwar, pro-Storey group vowing that if the *Times* fell, the *Tribune* would fall with it. "At this hour," one New York *Herald* dispatch ended, "the *Tribune* still stands." A vicious attack on Mrs. O'Leary was one of Storey's last flings; the Fire broke his nerve; he gave up the paper in 1878 and died insane. In 1891, Carter Harrison I bought the *Times* to have an organ to support his campaign to become "World's Fair Mayor." Four years later it was consolidated with the *Herald*.

In an over-all view, however, the *Tribune* and the *Daily News*, published by Victor Lawson, at the beginning in association with Melville E. Stone, have been the most important papers, and in the early days the *News* had the larger circulation. It began in 1876 as a penny paper (the *Tribune* cost five cents), specializing in brief, local items; it was not until the Spanish War that it began to build up its famous foreign news service. So few pennies were used in the seventies that arrangements were made with the mint to ship them in, and Stone persuaded merchants to mark goods 99¢ and $1.49. Advertisements were cut down and sometimes refused to avoid encroaching on news space. For religious reasons, the paper refused to publish a Sunday edition and rejected advertising for liquor, tobacco, firearms, burlesque shows, and harmful patent medicines. In the early days, their strike reporting was fairer than that of other papers, though Stone himself played an important part in sending the anarchists to the gallows. They conducted private detective campaigns to bring criminals to justice and in some cases led raids to enforce the law. They established clubrooms for newsboys and a sanitarium for sick children in Lincoln Park. They agitated for postal savings banks and took a straw vote in the 1896 presidential campaign. In the nineties the *News* distributed 1,500,000 copies of cheaply printed standard books and sponsored a "Home Study Circle" and a free public lecture series. Lord Northcliffe described their morning edition—first called the *Morning News*, then the *Record*—as his model for the London *Daily Mail*, and the *News* itself as the best afternoon paper in the world.

The *Record*, however, did not thrive. It became the *Record-Herald*, which, in the days of my youth, had "Buster Brown" and "Little Nemo" and a fine Sunday fiction magazine, and at one time it was owned by Herman H. Kohlsaat. In 1914, James Keeley, having left the *Tribune*, obtained possession of both it and the *Inter-Ocean*, naming the combined paper the *Herald*, but four years later he was obliged to sell it to Hearst, and it became the *Herald-Examiner*. Hearst's own Chicago beginnings go back to 1900, when he produced the *American* overnight, to support Bryan for president. Two years later, he added a morning paper, the *Examiner*. Kohlsaat also owned the *Inter-Ocean* at one time; so did Yerkes; but J. Young Scammon had founded it in 1872 as a paper "Republican in everything, Independent in nothing." Despite its checkered history, it was a handsome and often dignified sheet, with excellent features; in 1892 it presented its Sunday readers with the first color printing done by a rotary press in America.

There were other Chicago papers which would be well worth writing about if space were available. Many people still fondly remember the *Journal*, whose demise in 1929 ended an eighty-four-year run, and still more the *Evening Post* (1893–1932), an offshoot of the *Herald*, more interested in literature and the arts than most of its contemporaries. A number of dramatic, literary, and musical critics have made their mark in Chicago, but they have never produced the "features" that sold the most papers. Probably the number one feature has been the comics, which bloomed in the wake of Hearst's invasion, introducing Chicago to such dignitaries as Foxy Grandpa, Happy Hooligan, Little Jimmy, and the Katzenjammer Kids. As a child, I could never understand why my elders looked down on the Hearst papers when their comics were so obviously superior to those of their rivals. Political cartoons in Chicago had begun as early as the seventies, and during the 1896 campaign McCutcheon's famous dog, whose exact significance, if he had one, remained a mystery, interested almost as many readers as the candidates. The big change in the comics began in the early twenties and was distinctly a Chicago phenomenon under the aegis of Joseph Medill Patterson. With "Gasoline Alley," "Little Orphan Annie," "Dick Tracy," and their successors, the staple ingredients ceased to be the pranks of small boys, and all the characteristics of the serial story appeared. Frank King's Skeezix was the first child ever allowed to grow up in the comics, the Katzenjammer Kids still having the same age today that was theirs in 1900.

The most famous Chicago "column" was probably Eugene Field's "Sharps and Flats" in the *News* in the eighties and nineties; among Field's many successors have been Bert Leston Taylor with "A Line o' Type or Two" in the *Tribune* and Keith Preston with "Periscope" in the *News,* in the days of my youth, and Howard Vincent O'Brien and Sydney J. Harris since. In World's Fair days, George Ade's "Stories of the Streets and of the Town," illustrated by McCutcheon, was a great feature in the *Record*. The great humorist Finley Peter Dunne worked on most of the Chicago papers at one time or another, and his "Mr. Dooley" was distinctly a Chicago institution (his original was a barkeeper in Dearborn Street). Up to the Spanish-American War, Mr. Dooley concerned himself largely with local issues, but with Dunne's all-out attack on American imperialism fame was won, and many of the localisms had to be weeded out to make the essays intelligible to a world audience.

"Magazine" features, especially in the Sunday papers—Chicago papers printed much fiction and gave away colored reproductions of standard or sentimental pictures, "suitable for framing"—and the development of personal services were introduced largely for their appeal to women, whom the earlier editors had neglected, though the *Tribune* had a "Home Department" as early as 1852. In 1875 it dared to tackle the emotional problems of young men and women, and early in the 1900's Laura Jean Libbey took over the advice to the lovelorn, while none other than Lillian Russell wrote on beauty and many allied subjects, advising women not to cross their legs, for example, both because it was unrefined and because it might cause appendicitis! Many features had a special appeal to children, like Seymour Eaton's "The Roosevelt Bears," which ran on Saturdays in the *Daily News*. The *Tribune's* "Bright Sayings of the Children," for which Patterson paid one dollar each, were directed primarily to parents, but the children had their innings in "The Bird Lover's League," conducted by "Aunty Bee," in which the present scribe had the honor of making his first appearance in print.

The *Post's* "Friday Literary Review," beginning in 1909, enlisted, first, Francis Hackett, then Floyd Dell, still later Llewellyn Jones. After 1916 book reviewing became important in the *News*, and Harry Hansen's book page there is well remembered. At this time the *News* had a remarkably literary staff, including Ben Hecht, Wallace Smith, Lloyd Lewis, Vincent Starrett, and others; for a long time, Carl Sandburg functioned as film critic. Succeeding the more genteel Mrs. Elia W. Peattie, Burton Rascoe conducted a valiant campaign in the *Tribune* in behalf of James Branch Cabell and other modern writers; after his departure, books were rather allowed to languish for a time, Fanny Butcher, despite her wide influence, not being given nearly as much space as she ought to have had. The *Sun* started out with an impressive literary supplement, obviously designed with one eye on the *New York Times Book Review*, but as time went on, it declined in proportion to the *Tribune's* rival section, which had begun less ambitiously. Ben Hecht's *Chicago Literary Times*, in 1923–24, might be described as representing the lunatic fringe of the new literary emancipation, a kind of printed equivalent of the activities of the Dill Pickle Club and other pre-beatniks of the near North Side.

If the Chicago magazine record is less impressive than that of the newspapers, it was not for lack of trying. As we have seen, the *Tribune* itself grew out of a literary paper. The *Western Magazine* (1845) was the first in magazine form. No fewer than seventy titles dated from the great seedtime of the Exposition.

One of the most ambitious early ventures was the *Lakeside Monthly* (1871), which, though it printed some fiction, was essentially a critical journal, edited by Francis Fisher Browne, better known for his much longer connection with the *Dial*. It stopped in 1873, though *Scribner's Monthly* wished to consolidate with it; having convinced Eastern editors that there was valuable material available in the Middle West, it had in a sense fulfilled its purpose. Farther off center was *America* (1888–91), edited by the upper-class, anti-Catholic, antiforeigner Slason Thompson, at first in collaboration with Hobart C. Chatfield-Taylor, who trained himself to write by filling its pages under various pseudonyms, when there was no money to pay contributors. Here Eugene Field's "Little Boy Blue" first appeared. The *Dial*, too, seems ultraconservative to modern readers, but it was important because it was a nonsectional, serious literary review, published in the West. It endured in Chicago from 1880 to 1915, then transferred itself to New York, went "modern" and "creative" with a vengeance, and expired in 1929.

Two other periodicals demand mention: the *Little Review* as a phenomenon and *Poetry: A Magazine of Verse* as a solid success. The former was published in Chicago from March, 1914, to December, 1916, then moved to New York. Once the pages which should have been devoted to creative writing were left blank because nothing worthy had been submitted. "It was the perfect flower of adolescence," says Eunice Tietjens, "the triumph of wide-eyed and high-hearted ineptitude. It was a blaze of courage and a mine of foolishness. It was delicious." The *Little Review* was the creation of a divinely mad girl named Margaret Anderson, who made up the first number from unread galleys because nobody had ever told her about proofreading. When they could not pay the rent of their house in Lake Bluff, Margaret, her sister, the sister's two boys, and their nurse moved out to three tents on the lake shore near Ravinia in April, but Margaret took her oriental rugs along. Yet they managed to get contributions from a large number of very distinguished writers.

There was none of Margaret Anderson's naïveté about Harriet Monroe, and none of her charm either. In World's Fair days she made up her mind that there must be a dedicatory ode, and that she must write it. Having had it accepted, she presented a bill for one thousand dollars, which, amazingly, was paid. She fought another battle to have it read at the exercises, which was achieved in part by Mrs. Le Moyne. But the printed editions of her masterpiece just would not sell. "Evidently the public for poetry had oozed away since the happy day when Longfellow received three thousand dollars for 'The Hanging of the Crane.'" She was aware that there was a difference in quality between the two poems, but this seemed to her all to her advantage; she had only contempt for Longfellow. As a matter of fact, she left him far behind commercially when the New York *World* printed the poem without authorization, and she sued and collected five thousand dollars, though they appealed the case as far as the Supreme Court. After this it ought to have been clear that Harriet was capable of promoting anything.

Poetry began with Chatfield-Taylor's suggestion that Miss Monroe get one hundred Chicagoans to subscribe fifty dollars a year for five years, and though a Philadelphia paper sneered at Chicago for using "the proceeds of pork for the promotion of poetry," it was a success from its establishment in 1912. "*Poetry* is my mother," wrote Amy Lowell exuberantly, calling Chicago "my adopted city" and "the city of my heart." "General William Booth Enters into Heaven," in January, 1913, established Vachel Lindsay, and Mrs. Carl Sandburg held the magazine responsible for bringing her husband back to the creative life after years of discouragement. From the beginning there were controversies about imagism and other isms, all of which had their commercial value. *Poetry* "discovered" Tagore, and gave a banquet for Yeats. I find it delightfully amusing that Joyce Kilmer's "Trees" should have become the most frequently reprinted poem that ever appeared in it, but with all Miss Monroe's limitations, the survival of the magazine and its establishment upon a firm business basis, even when she is no longer on hand to guide it, certainly stand on the credit side of the Chicago ledger.

III

What is Chicago literature? Is it literature about Chicago, or is it literature written by Chicago writers? For that matter, what is a Chicago writer? and what is to be done with those who are born and reared in Chicago and then move away? or those others who come from elsewhere, are touched by the city's influence, and depart? Frank Norris spent his first fifteen years in Chicago, and *The Pit* (1903) is certainly an important Chicago novel, but it is inferior to *The Octopus* and *McTeague*, neither of which have anything to do with the Midwest metropolis. Finally, what is to be said of casual visitors like George Gissing, who spent six months in Chicago in 1877 and supported himself by writing fiction for the *Tribune*. "I have never come across an English editor," wrote that unhappy man, "who treated me with anything like that consideration and general kindness."

These questions are interesting but inconclusive and not strictly apropos, for certainly no complete history of literature in Chicago can be undertaken in this section. According to Lennox Bouton Grey, who in 1935 produced a magnificent doctoral dissertation for the University of Chicago on the theme of "The Great American Novel," between four and five hundred novels about Chicago had by then been written by more than two hundred writers.

Special aspects of Chicago history have been used again and again—Fort Dearborn, the Fire, the Haymarket affair, the World's Columbian Exposition, etc.—sometimes in works devoted entirely to these subjects, sometimes incidentally in novels of wider scope. E. P. Roe, who was not a Chicagoan, began his spectacular career as popular fictionist with *Barriers Burned Away* (1872), which, though not a work of quality, is remarkable for its refusal to take up the anti-art point of view then so characteristic of extreme evangelicals. Frank Harris, in *The Bomb* (1909), presented Chicago with an East Side and winter weather "for weeks together . . . from ten to forty degrees below zero" because of "great frozen lakes [which] surround it to the north"! All these themes except Fort Dearborn weave in and out of Robert Herrick's fictions. In *Chimes* (1926),

Herrick painted a hostile picture of the University of Chicago, where he taught. Mr. Grey has observed that novels about academicians are more searchingly critical, or at least self-critical, than the more numerous novels about businessmen, and that Northwestern has in general inspired a more romantic kind of novel than Chicago, though with *Bertram Cope's Year* (1929) by Henry B. Fuller formed of elements drawn from both institutions. Charles T. Yerkes appears in many novels besides Dreiser's *The Financier* (1912), *The Titan* (1914), and *The Stoic* (1947), in which he is the central figure. Will Payne wrote of the newspaperman in *Jerry the Dreamer* (1896), as did Samuel Merwin and Henry Kitchell Webster at a later date, but none of these novels are now as well known as the tough play by Ben Hecht and Charles MacArthur, *The Front Page* (1928). Newspapermen have not always written about themselves. Stanley Waterloo's best-known book was a cave-man story, *The Story of Ab* (1897), much admired by Theodore Roosevelt; he also did a book called *Armageddon: A Tale of Love, War, and Invention* (1898), in which a Christian peace was inaugurated after a great war and sustained by bombing airships built in Chicago! Opie Read, too, was a newspaperman, but even when he wrote of the city, he retained the rural humorist's point of view.

In *The Social Lion* (1899), published under the pseudonym Robert Dolly Williams, the seventeen-year-old Margaret Horton Potter achieved an exposé of Chicago society from the inside, with *roman à clef* characters. The first edition was sold out in two weeks, and the Potter family suppressed the book, though it was later reprinted. Theodore Dreiser's *Sister Carrie* (1900) is only in part a Chicago novel, but it fairly drips the atmosphere of the Union Park district and the sporting and theatrical life of the city. Willa

Cather's *The Song of the Lark* (1915) and *Lucy Gayheart* (1935) have only episodes in Chicago, but Theodore Thomas, the Art Institute, and the life of the music studios come vividly to life in them. Arthur Meeker divides himself as novelist between Chicago and Europe and made his first big strike with *The Ivory Mischief* (1941), which is set in Louis XIV's France, but *Prairie Avenue* (1949) is a successful evocation of the spirit of "the sunny street that holds the sifted few," and *The Far-Away Music* (1945), which goes back to the fifties and involves family memories, is a truly radiant piece of writing. Yet the characteristic type of "Chicago novel" would seem to be that which traces the development of a family through three generations or more, and, as Grey says, has been cultivated mainly by women, who have "leaned as social matriarchs in their masculine city, towards heroines of dynamic, almost masculine temperaments." Early examples would be Edna Ferber's *The Girls* (1921) and, with variations, Edgar Lee Masters' *Children of the Market Place* (1922), but for the full development we must go to Janet Ayer Fairbank *(The Smiths*, 1925; etc.) and her sister, Margaret Ayer Barnes *(Years of Grace*, 1930; *Within This Present*, 1933; etc.), and to Ruth Russell's impressionistic and beautifully wrought *Lake Front* (1931), which covers the whole span from Marquette to the gangster era.

Women had been important in the Chicago novel ever since Juliette (Mrs. John A.) Kinzie, of the pioneer family, had published *Wau-Ban: The Early Day in the Northwest* in 1856. Caroline M. Kirkland concerned herself with Chicago and other midwestern locales in *Western Clearings* (1845) and other books, and her son, Joseph Kirkland, who importantly influenced Hamlin Garland, treated three different periods in *Zury* (1887), *The McVeys* (1888), and

The Captain of Company K (1890). Like many later novels, Martha J. Lamb's now scarce and almost forgotten *Spicy* (1873) uses the past to place her Chicago present in perspective. The romantic Mary Hartwell Catherwood, on the other hand, was primarily interested in preserving, with "sincere" and "truthful" "love and gratitude," what she regarded as the cherishable heritage which the French had left in the Midwest, in whose defense she was prepared to oppose the "veritism" of Hamlin Garland and others who seemed to her to be concerning themselves with less idealistic themes.

Yet surely Garland was idealistic enough, for all the iconoclasm of *Crumbling Idols* (1894), and passion itself is beautiful in his most important Chicago novel, *Rose of Dutcher's Coolly* (1895), which shocked the prudish in its time. Howells agreed with him that the Chicago renascence which was in the making would be an important one; the Englishman Walter Besant saw Chicago as a great world center; even Henry Adams and Charles Eliot Norton were hopeful. But neither boasting nor exuberance appeared in the Chicago novelists who seemed most representative of their time, like the now forgotten Hobart C. Chatfield-Taylor in the nineties *(With Edge Tools; An American Peeress; Two Women and a Fool)* and Robert Herrick and Henry B. Fuller a little later. By his own statement, Herrick's principal preoccupation was the corrupting influence of the competitive system. This corruption he studied in the packer in *The Memoirs of an American Citizen* (1905); in the financier in *A Life for a Life* (1910); in the architect and the engineer in *The Common Lot* (1904) and *Waste* (1924); in the painter in *One Woman's Life* (1913); in the physician in *The Man Who Wins* (1897), *The Web of Life* (1900), and *The Healer* (1911). And since sex is the only other force in life as strong as "the spirit of possession," there are women everywhere, sometimes another influence for corruption and sometimes quite the reverse. Humanly and technically, Herrick's books are curious combinations of strength and weakness, but as acerbic as his tone often is, he was basically an idealist, and no writer was ever more representative of the novel of social criticism in Chicago. Henry B. Fuller's women are perhaps more predatory, and he himself was an even lonelier figure than Herrick. He hated Chicago; he probably would have liked to devote all his writing time to such books as *The Chevalier of Pensieri-Vani* (1890), which both Lowell and Norton greatly admired. But it was *The Cliff-Dwellers* (1893), a perfect title for a novel about a city of skyscrapers, *With the Procession* (1895), and *On the Stairs* (1918) which drew him into the novelistic main stream and won from Dreiser his acknowledgment of indebtedness.

Obviously not all Chicago writers have written much about Chicago. Ernest Hemingway, for example, did not; though he was born and grew up in Oak Park, only his childhood summers in Michigan seem to have given him any literary material, and all his best-known books have foreign or exotic backgrounds. Nor, to go to the other extreme, were local influences any more important in the work of his senior Oak Parker, Edgar Rice ("Tarzan") Burroughs, nor in that of John McCutcheon's brother, George Barr McCutcheon, whose *Graustark* series created a dream world on the model of *The Prisoner of Zenda*.

Chicago had a great poet, and in lesser measure playwright, in Herrick's colleague, William Vaughn Moody, who, if he had not died at forty, might have become one of the greatest of all American poets. Indiana-born and Harvard-trained, Moody was essentially a cosmopolitan, but

I think there can be no doubt that, much as he thought he disliked it, his Chicago residence made him a less "literary" writer than he would otherwise have been and brought him in touch with more vital themes. The local note is much stronger, however, in the poets of the World War I revival who have already been mentioned in connection with *Poetry*. Masters, Lindsay, and Sandburg were all born in Illinois, though not in Chicago, yet they all saw a good deal of the city. Masters had the closest ties, for he was a successful Chicago lawyer when *Spoon River Anthology*, serialized not in *Poetry* but in *Reedy's Mirror* of St. Louis, appeared in 1915. He had already published a number of obscure books and contributed to many newspapers in Chicago and elsewhere, including Eugene Field's "Sharps and Flats" column in the *Daily News*. Yet even Masters departed for the East as soon as it became clear that he was going to be able to live on literature. Another important figure of this revival who was not a poet, Sherwood Anderson, was born in Ohio, but lived in Chicago in his teens and again after giving up business to become a writer, when he was encouraged by such diverse figures as Robert Morss Lovett and Ben Hecht. Though he is not essentially a Chicago writer, Chicago furnishes the setting for *Windy McPherson's Son* (1916) and *Marching Men* (1917). The poet Kenneth Fearing was born in Oak Park, and more recently the Negro, Pultizer Prize–winning poet Gwendolyn Brooks has reflected credit upon herself and her race.

In Chicago as elsewhere, recent writers have been discovering what every small boy always knew—that there are some nasty words in the English language and that these nasty words are the products of nasty minds; consequently there has been a tendency to turn to the bottom rather than the top for what it now seems quaint to describe as literary inspiration. Thus Nelson Algren, of *The Neon Wilderness* (1947) and *The Man with the Golden Arm* (1949) tells us that "the more I see of those below, the more I say the hell with you squares on top," to which I suppose one can only reply, " 'Everybody to his own taste,' as the old lady said when she kissed the cow." Willard Motley's *Knock on Any Door* (1947) concerns a juvenile delinquent who dies in the electric chair. James T. Farrell, of the *Studs Lonigan* trilogy, has been concerned mainly with the South Side Irish, and Meyer Levin, of *The Old Bunch* (1937), etc., with the Jews who grew up in the Nineteenth Ward and were pushed out by changing circumstances. Albert Halper, born in Chicago, did not begin to publish until after his removal to New York, but *The Chute* (1929), *The Foundry* (1934), and other novels have a Chicago industrial background. I do not mean to imply, however, that all writers who choose such themes lack either merit or even idealism; this depends entirely on the character of what they turn out. And in case the reader has not yet discovered it, this may be a good point at which to remind him that the writer of this book does not know everything about Chicago, and that everything the reader himself may wish to know about it will not necessarily be found within these pages.

7

I

THE first regular dramatic performances in Chicago were given at the Sauganash Hotel in 1837. Next year there was a Chicago Theater on Dearborn Street, but the first important theater was that erected by the future mayor John B. Rice at Randolph and Dearborn in 1847. Rice's best seats cost fifty cents, and to keep prostitutes out, "females" were not admitted unless accompanied by "a gentleman." The main item on the opening bill was *The Four Sisters*, a farce with the future Mrs. John Drew, grandmother of the Barrymores, in the cast. In those days, not even *Hamlet* could fill out a bill, though Chicago saw all the famous Hamlets, sometimes with rivals exhibiting themselves at rival theaters simultaneously.

Rice's second theater, 1851, cost $11,000, but James H. McVicker spent $85,000 on his first theater, opened in Madison Street on November 5, 1857, and Uranus H. Crosby's Opera House on Washington Street cost $600,000 in 1866. Both houses burned, of course, in 1871. There were three McVicker's legitimate theaters on the same site; the last declined to vaudeville before, in 1922, it was pulled down to be replaced by the motion picture theater which perpetuates its name. McVicker, himself a gifted and wistful comedian of the Joseph Jefferson order, was the father of Edwin Booth's second wife, and it was on his stage that a madman, one night in 1879, fired a pistol at Booth; the actor had the bullet dug out of the scenery and wore it, mounted, on his watch chain, inscribed "From Mark Gray to Edwin Booth." Here, too, Sarah Bernhardt played her first Chicago engagement, in January, 1881, in *Phèdre*, *Camille*, etc., accompanied by much asinine discussion as to whether she was a proper person to meet or even to see, all of which she was too generous to mention when she wrote her memoirs. Crosby's Opera House had a checkered history. Its opening was postponed because of the assassination of Lincoln, and in 1868, General Grant was nominated there for the presidency. In financial difficulties in 1867, Crosby auctioned it off, to enormous interest and widespread suspicion of skulduggery, not allayed by the fact that the unknown winner, A. H. Lee of Prairie du Rocher, "sold" it back to him after winning it. Richard Hooley's first theater was on Clark Street, on the site later occupied by the Grand. After the Fire he built the theater on Randolph Street later known as Powers', which, at least until the Blackstone was opened, was regarded as Chicago's most aristocratic house. It opened unaristocratically enough with *The Black Crook*, but Daly, Daniel Frohman, and Belasco all showed Chicago their productions there, and it remained important until the twenties, when the Hotel Sherman gobbled up its space, Otis Skinner in *Sancho Panza* being the closing attraction. Harry Powers was also involved in the handsome Illinois, on Jackson between Wabash and Michigan, which was wantonly destroyed to make room for a parking lot.

There could be no point in enumerating the actors who played in Chicago; all actors played there. "Chicago," Shaw wrote Ellen Terry in 1900, when she was touring in America, "is a comparatively enlightened town; my plays get

145

good houses there." In the old days there were many more "firsts" in Chicago than there are today. Sothern and Marlowe first played together, at the Illinois Theater, on September 19, 1904. There was comedy in 1902, when a Chicago real estate man, Samuel E. Gross, got a legal judgment to the effect that Rostand had stolen *Cyrano de Bergerac* from him, and in 1889 and following there were melodrama and filth and ultimately tragedy in the Leslie Carter divorce suit. It was at Carter Harrison's home that Louise Dudley, a Kentuckian, had met her husband-to-be; it was a black day for him. After the divorce she got Belasco to make a star of her; she must be very nearly the only American woman who ever built a career on a scandal.

In the early days not all the theaters were in the Loop; before the decline of the neighborhood, both the Academy of Music and the Haymarket, in the vicinity of Madison and Halsted, were respected houses, and the Haymarket occasionally played second-rate traveling companies into my childhood. There were many foreign-language theatricals: the Garrick Theater, designed by Louis Sullivan, and but recently destroyed, was originally the Schiller, decorated with bas-relief portraits of great Germans, and Glickman's Palace, on Blue Island Avenue at Roosevelt Road, was long devoted to the Yiddish drama. Before the movies ran them out, there were stock companies all over Chicago; the one I knew best was at the People's, at Van Buren and Leavitt, where, for a number of years, the splendid Marie Nelson, a classical type of the old-time stock actress, famous in her own bailiwick and practically unknown elsewhere, acted practically everything, putting on a new play every Monday night and giving Tuesday, Thursday, Saturday, and Sunday matinees. (She died in Chicago in 1943.) A little later, West Siders were going to the Imperial, at Madison and Western, to see Eda von Luke; and Bob Casey has celebrated the charms of Howard's and the Criterion on the North Side, where Lincoln J. Carter devoted himself to "the melodramas that were to the theater of the day what the comic strip is to current literature." Fortunately, however, melodrama was not confined to such theaters. Not only in Chicago but in all large cities such plays as *The Round Up, In Old Kentucky, The Old Homestead*, and *Way Down East* were annual visitors, and people went to see them year after year, more enthralled by the spectacular scenic effects they had accumulated than by the virtues of the script.

The most famous Little Theater in Chicago was the one which Maurice Browne and his wife, Ellen Van Volkenburg, operated in a little auditorium seating ninety-one persons in the Fine Arts Building, between 1912 and 1917. Later, in London, they produced *Journey's End* and other successful plays. Miss Van Volkenburg, a gifted actress as well as a superb director, has also functioned as a distinguished teacher of actors, and the late Gilmor Brown of the Pasadena Playhouse is said to have named her and Edith Wynne Matthison as the two finest actresses in America, pointing out that neither was appearing on the professional stage. Because of its great influence, the Chicago Little Theater is often spoken of as the first such institution in America. It was not; as Browne himself scrupulously pointed out in his autobiography, *Too Late to Lament* (1956), he was preceded in Chicago by Laura Dainty Pelham and the Hull-House Players; he might also have mentioned the work of Anna Morgan, which went back to the nineties. Both Browne and Miss Morgan were essentially "art theater" people, concerning themselves with forward-looking but not freakish playwrights neglected by the commercial theater. Neither, however, was exclusively contemporary-minded. Miss Morgan produced Browning's *In a Balcony* before Mrs. LeMoyne discovered it, and one of the great Little Theater achievements was the production of *The Trojan Women*, timed to protest against the madness of World War I. The Hull-House Players favored more socially oriented drama. Later little theaters included the Jack and Jill and the Studio Players on the near North Side, which first produced in the city such plays as *The Adding Machine* and *All God's Chillun Got Wings*.

The theater business has many fringes. As early as 1834 a humble predecessor of such later great magicians as Hermann and Thurston advertised an entertainment at the Mansion House during which he "would draw a red hot poker across his tongue, and would eat fire balls, hot sealing wax, live coals and melted lead." In the sixties there was Wood's Museum in Randolph Street, with "150,000 curiosities of every kind"; later Chicagoans went to the Eden Musée, which included a chamber of horrors. Circuses, Wild West shows, etc. touched the edges of the later organized sports world; there were four baseball teams by 1860, and the "White Stockings" date back to 1870. In view of the later popularity of the movies, it is interesting that "Optical Illusions and Dissolving Views" were among the very early entertainments offered in Chicago. In the nineties there were cycloramas in Wabash Avenue, devoted to such subjects as *The Battle of Gettysburg*, *The Great Chicago Fire*, and *The Crucifixion*, and I myself can remember such spectacles as *The Battle of the Monitor and the Merrimac* and *The Creation*, both presented at Riverview, the only present survivor of Chicago's once numerous amusement parks, the latter in a building especially constructed for it, with a huge plaster angel holding it up and spreading out his wings over its full exterior width. As for vaudeville, it was all over the city, and for a long time it supplemented movies, even in the five-cent theaters, which, if they did not have vaudeville, were pretty sure to have an "illustrated song," sung to the accompaniment of colored slides.

Much nonsense has been written about Chicago having once been the movie capital of America. It never was, but it was a very important film trading center, and it had two important film companies—Selig and Essanay, both of whom also produced in California. The Chicago historians tend to overlook Selig—whose *The Adventures of Kathlyn* (1913–14), produced in collaboration with the *Tribune*, marked the real beginnings of the movie serial—and to overestimate Essanay, probably because Chaplin worked for them. But he made only one picture in Chicago—*His New Job* (1915)—after which he moved on to the Coast. The "Broncho Billy" pictures were made in California too, but Francis X. Bushman, Gloria Swanson, Wallace Beery, and others were an authentic part of the Chicago movie scene. Walt Disney was a Chicagoan of course, and both D. W. Griffith and Mary Pickford saw their first films in Chicago. *Photoplay Magazine* began publication in Chicago in 1912 and remained there for many years, and Louella Parsons pioneered movie-gossip journalism there.

How much is left of the legitimate theater in Chicago today? Well, how much is left of it anywhere? By 1960, Claudia Cassidy could begin her annual piece on "The Season in Chicago" for the *Best Plays* annual by asking "What season in Chicago?" Four theaters had operated—one forty-four weeks, one twenty-nine and one-half, one twenty-two, and one ten. In the 1955–56 season there had been six, their figures respectively thirty-eight, thirty-six, thirty-three, twenty-seven, eleven, and five, and in 1951–52 it had been eight, running fifty-two, fifty-one and one-half, twenty-seven, seventeen, thirteen, eleven, thirteen and one-half, and two. Yet there are curious contradictions to be observed. While Chicago does not get nearly so many productions as Boston and other tryout towns closer to New York, it can still achieve immensely longer runs, and *The Music Man* grossed $3,250,000 there. Two of Tennessee Williams' plays —*The Glass Menagerie* and *The Night of the Iguana*—were produced in Chicago; so was *A Raisin in the Sun*. The city has recently acquired a huge, new, handsome theater in McCormick Place on the lake front, and there is still hope that the Auditorium may be restored. Night club and cabaret theaters thrive—throwing up such new personalities as Shelley Berman and Mike and Elaine—and summer theaters sometimes threaten to develop into all-year-round affairs. The Civic Theater more or less collapsed with the Civic Opera, but the Art Institute's Goodman Theater can still achieve fine productions like the recent *Passage to India* with Lillian Gish. All this makes more unanswerable the question which has been asked again and again: Why in the world does the city not cut its New York apron strings and itself produce plays for Chicago and the Middle West?

II

Music in Chicago may have begun with Mark Beaubien's fiddle at the old Sauganash Tavern; in 1834 Jean Beaubien is supposed to have brought in the first piano, and a Negro named Wilson P. Perry advertised his willingness to supply music for parties. According to George P. Upton, the first quartet choir was organized at St. James Church in 1836 and the first organ installed there, and in 1848 Richard Hoffman became the first distinguished pianist to perform in the city. Chicago's first orchestra, the Philharmonic Society, directed by Julius Dyhrenfurth, dedicated Tremont Hall in 1850. After the Fire, lectures and concerts were given in the Union Park Congregational Church and other West Side buildings, until in 1879 the Central Music Hall was built where Marshall Field's now stands and remained the focus of the musical life of the city until the Auditorium was opened in 1889. Important choral organizations were the Beethoven Society (1873), the Mozart Society (1881), and the Apollo Club (1872), which still flourishes.

   Theodore Thomas had been in and out of the city for some time; in the summer of 1887 he gave a series of fifty concerts in the Exposition Building on the lake front. But the idea of bringing him to Chicago permanently began with Norman Fay's question "Would you come to Chicago if we would give you a permanent orchestra?" to which Thomas replied, "I would go to hell if they gave me a permanent orchestra." Fay's first idea was to get ten men to subscribe five thousand dollars a year for three years, but Marshall Field shrewdly suggested that interest would be greater if fifty men gave one thousand dollars each. The first concert was in the Auditorium, October 17, 1891; the program included Beethoven's *Fifth*, Wagner's *Faust* overture, and Dvořák's *Husitzká*. The deficit looked so bad at first that Thomas was sure the first season would be the last, but he refused an offer from Boston because he thought he had no right to leave Chicago in the lurch, and the guarantors stood by him nobly, both then and afterwards. In 1900–1901 he ventured upon a series of four concerts devoted to Beethoven alone, which were well attended and received; later there was an historical cycle of six programs illustrating the evolution of orchestral music. When Richard Strauss functioned as guest conductor in 1904, he found that for "beauty of tone, technical perfection and discipline" the orchestra had surpassed his highest expectations, and that to rehearse with such men was "no labor but a great pleasure."

But Thomas thought the Auditorium too big for orchestral concerts (his programs were broken in upon by other bookings, and since people knew that seats would always be available, they would not buy season tickets), and finally he insisted upon the erection of Orchestra Hall. The sum of $750,000 was raised, and Daniel H. Burnham designed the building according to Thomas's own ideas. It was dedicated on December 14, 1904, with a program comprising Beethoven's *Fifth*, *Tod und Verklärung*, the "Hallelujah Chorus," and "Hail! Bright Abode" from *Tannhäuser*. But tragedy mingled with triumph. The hall was cold and drafty, and damp from undried plaster; Thomas took a chill, collapsed just before Christmas, and died on Friday morning, January 4. "I have had a beautiful vision," he told his wife, "a beautiful vision." A memorial service on Sunday afternoon packed the Auditorium, with crowds standing outside in the streets in tribute to the great musician. The orchestra was handed over to the assistant conductor, Frederick Stock, who remained a beloved and dominating figure in the musical life of the city until his death in 1942. Two subsequent conductors had considerable difficulty pleasing Claudia Cassidy, but under Fritz Reiner everybody seems to have been happy.

Chicago's first opera was *La Sonnambula*, at Rice's Theater, July 29, 1850. (The theater burned the second night.) In 1885 there was a big festival in the Exposition Building, involving Colonel James Henry Mapleson, Patti, and Luigi Arditi as conductor. On September 29, 1895, the Castle Square Opera Company of Boston opened the Studebaker in the Fine Arts Building with a performance of *Faust* in

English; for some years, this theater was known as the home of English opera, light opera, and musical comedy. The first opera given in the Auditorium, December 10, 1889, was Gounod's *Romeo et Juliette*, with Patti; when, on January 26, 1929, the Chicago Civic Opera Company deserted the building for Samuel Insull's new Civic Opera House on the river, Edith Mason and Charles Hackett appeared in the same work.

Until 1910, Chicago depended for its opera on visits from the Metropolitan and other companies. One week in 1890, Lilli Lehmann sang a *Masked Ball* on Monday, *Fidelio* on Wednesday, and *Norma* on Friday. Schumann-Heink made her Metropolitan debut in Chicago, November 7, 1898, as Ortrud in *Lohengrin*, and it was in the Auditorium, in April 1909, that Geraldine Farrar and Arturo Toscanini, hitherto at swords-points concerning the respective importance of prima donnas and conductors, made up their quarrel and announced their reconciliation by taking a joint curtain call.

Then in 1910, Chicago's own opera company was organized, with Cleofonte Campanini as musical director and first conductor, and with artists drawn largely from Hammerstein's disbanded Manhattan Opera, plus a number of top guest stars from the Metropolitan. *Aïda* was sung the first night, November 3. At the Saturday matinee, November 5, Mary Garden, who above all other artists was to personify Chicago opera, appeared in her greatest role, Mélisande, which was quickly followed by Louise, Thaïs, and Salomé, the sensation of the season, which involved the police, the Chicago Law and Order League, and other custodians of public morals, and led to the Strauss opera's being banned in Chicago, and to a number of rather pointed remarks from Miss Garden and others concerning musical illiteracy. On December 27, Carolina White, just beginning a short-lived musical celebrity, appeared in the Emmy Destinn role in Chicago's own production of Puccini's new opera, *The Girl of the Golden West* (Caruso later dropped in from the Metropolitan to sing in one performance).

The brilliant and ill-starred Gerville-Réache sang two first nights in the second season (1911–12), appearing first as Dalila and then as Carmen, substituting for Miss Garden, who was ill. Maggie Teyte, a mite of a young prima donna among some overwhelming colleagues, sang the title role in Massenet's *Cendrillon* (for many years there was a painting of her in her ballroom dress in the Fine Arts Building), with Garden as the Prince. Garden also added *Le Jongleur de Notre Dame* to her repertoire, and on December 13 she served the desperate cause of opera in English by appearing with White and George Hamlin in Victor Herbert's *Natoma*. Finally, on January 12, Miss White won the greatest triumph of her career in Wolf-Ferrari's *The Jewels of the Madonna*, an opera which Chicago alone seems ever greatly to have loved.

Titta Ruffo made a sensational debut as Rigoletto during the 1912–13 season, and the next year brought Florence Macbeth, Lucien Muratore (with whom Garden sang in *Monna Vanna* and much besides), and Rosa Raisa, loved for her opulence of voice and kindliness of spirit to the end of the Civic Opera chapter in Chicago, and thereafter, with her husband, Giacomo Rimini, as a distinguished teacher of singing. There was no season in 1914–15, for the company was bankrupt, but it was reorganized by Harold McCormick and others. On Saturday afternoon, November 18, 1916, Chicago (and the world) discovered Galli-Curci, and the S.R.O. sign was out thereafter for every performance she sang. Campanini died on December 19, 1919, and was given a public funeral on a stage set for the Transformation

Scene in *Parsifal;* the orchestra played the Prelude from Saint-Saëns' *The Deluge*, and Raisa sang the "Inflammatus" from Rossini's *Stabat Mater*. Later Giorgio Polacco became musical director. Tito Schipa and Edward Johnson came in during the 1919–20 season, and in January, 1921, Mary Garden was elected general director, remaining in charge through the following artistically brilliant but financially disastrous season, and running up a deficit of $1,100,000, which Harold McCormick cheerfully paid. On Armistice Day, 1921, the first opera *(Butterfly* with Edith Mason) was broadcast, but was heard only by a few hundred amateurs with crystal sets. The company reorganized itself again in January, 1922, with Samuel Insull as president, now calling itself the Chicago Civic Opera Company. The new Civic Opera House, which was supposed to put opera on a business basis by paying deficits out of business rentals, began with the prime opener, *Aïda*, on November 4, 1929, and the company remained there until the depression put it out of business in 1932.

In the days of its glory, the Chicago Opera Company reached heights which made it seem reasonable to compare it to the Metropolitan, Miss Garden's presence rendering it especially distinguished in the French section. It seems odd that a city with so small a French population should have done so well with French art at the Art Institute and French music at the opera house, and it seems even more odd that Miss Garden should have cared so little for Massenet, in whose operas she spent so much of her stage time. She sang *Salomé* in French; as a matter of fact, she did *Tosca* in French too, when she was compelled to do it at all, the rest of the cast singing Italian, except for the "Vissi d'arte," which, for some reason, she preferred to do in the language of the composer. She was "Our Mary" in Chicago, but she was a world figure too; there were other, less famous singers who seemed to belong to us more peculiarly. Such an one was Irene Pavloska, whose vocal resources were not outstandingly opulent but whose sense of character was unsurpassed. Her Hänsel was sheer mischievous delight, her Suzuki the purest unselfish devotion. When she sang Lola in *Cavalleria Rusticana* she had the wanton allure of every shameless woman in the world in the least flick of her impudent red skirt, and as Kupava in *The Snow Maiden* she could melt the hardest heart. Nor must I forget that at least one sweet romance came out of the Chicago Opera. In 1926, Claire Dux married Charles Swift and lived with him happily as a distinguished member of the Chicago community until his death more than twenty years later.

Some singers—Miss Garden for one—did not relish leaving the Auditorium, which was as distinguished accoustically as architecturally. I wonder how many Chicagoans used to sit through the intermissions as I did, gazing at the famous mural over the proscenium arch, so suggestive of the pilgrimage of man, and the names of the illustrious composers in raised gold letters running clear down to the stage, or examining those other murals, halfway back, with the mottoes: "O soft melodious Springtime, first-born of life and love" and "A great life has passed into the tomb, and there awaits the requiem of winter's snows." Of course the great hall was used for concerts as well as opera, and in the old days Chicago was a great concert center, nearly all the recitals being given, for some strange reason, at the same hour on Sunday afternoon. I remember one Sunday when Clara Butt was singing in Cohan's Grand against Geraldine Farrar in the Auditorium, who was followed, a few hours later, in the same theater, by Galli-Curci. Among composers, Carrie Jacobs-Bond and Reginald de Koven had their Chicago connections, and later there was John Alden Carpenter, whose ballet, *The Birthday of the Infanta*, was staged at the Civic Opera. George Hamlin pioneered in bringing out songs by Richard Strauss, Hugo Wolf, Max Reger, and others, and we did not fail to appreciate the great pianist Fannie Bloomfield Zeisler because she was an established part of the Chicago scene. From 1908 on until the Patten Gymnasium was torn down to make room for Northwestern's Technological Institute, there was a great North Shore Music Festival in Evanston, and in the twenties and up to 1931, Louis Eckstein used to manage a ten-week opera season of his own at Ravinia Park on the North Shore, now the summer home of the Chicago Symphony Orchestra.

After the collapse of the Civic Opera, Chicago was again without its own opera until 1954. Then the famous "I Will" spirit embodied itself for the time being in a young lady named Carol Fox, who, enlisting the aid of a real estate man, Lawrence Kelly, and a conductor named Nicola Rescigno, formed the Lyric Theater (now the Lyric Opera). In February, 1954, they presented two "calling card" performances of *Don Giovanni*, with Steber, Sayao, Rossi-Lemeni, Simoneau, and others, and in the fall their first three-week season was glorified by the American debut of Maria Callas in *Norma*, *La Traviata*, and *Lucia*. From that not-too-modest beginning, Lyric Opera has now worked itself up to an eight-week season on a paying basis, having achieved the all-time miracle of selling out 96.7 per cent of its entire seating capacity for the whole 1962–63 season. By this time, too, they had presented 244 performances of fifty-five works. Practically all contemporary opera singers of distinction have now appeared with the Lyric Opera, Simionato, Gobbi, and Tebaldi having come again and again.

Teresa Stich-Randall, Anna Moffo, Gré Brouwenstijn, Renata Scotto, Walter Berry, Carlo Bergonzi, Michel Roux, Hans Hotter, and Eberhard Waechter made their first American operatic appearances in Chicago, and Tebaldi sang her first American *Butterfly*, *Falstaff*, and *Andrea Chenier* there, Nilsson her first Isolde and her first Verdi. Both Joan Sutherland and Leontyne Price appeared with the Lyric Opera before being heard at the Metropolitan, and Elisabeth Schwartzkopf has not yet appeared at the New York house. A number of interesting novelties have been presented, including the Czech opera *Jenufa*. The company inaugurated the policy of renting productions from opera houses across the world, thus not only reducing expenses but permitting viewers a much wider range of *décor* than would otherwise have been possible. In 1958 they received a subsidy of sixteen thousand dollars from the Italian government, which has also decorated Miss Fox. All in all, it has been an amazing record, of which both Chicago and the management may well be proud, and which augurs well for the future.

III

The museums of Chicago do not all relate to the arts, nor can they all be considered here. The Art Institute and the Chicago Natural History Museum (formerly known as the Field Museum) are on the lake front, along with the Adler Planetarium and Astronomical Museum and the John G. Shedd Aquarium. The headquarters of the Chicago Historical Society and the Museum of Natural History maintained by the Chicago Academy of Sciences, which specializes in the natural history of the Chicago area, are in Lincoln Park, and, as has already been indicated, the Museum of Science and Industry occupies the restored Fine Arts Building in Jackson Park.

Art in Chicago is not identical with the Art Institute, though there is a powerful temptation to consider it so. The sculptor Leonard Volk and the painter G. P. A. Healy both came in the fifties. Healy painted the portraits of all the prominent Chicagoans of his time, and one of the most amusing anecdotes of the Fire concerns Mrs. D. L. Moody's vain attempt to get her husband out into the street burdened with his own portrait! Even today not all the art treasures are in the museum; there are murals by Jules Guerin in the Illinois Merchants Trust Bank, windows designed by Burne-Jones and executed by William Morris in the Second Presbyterian Church, and much besides. The Chicago Academy of Design, founded in 1866, was reorganized after the Fire as the Chicago Academy of Fine Arts; in 1882 it became the Art Institute of Chicago. That same year it moved from rented quarters at State and Monroe to the southwest corner of Michigan and Van Buren, where in 1887 a Romanesque building designed by John W. Root was opened. This, however, was soon outgrown, and after the World's Columbian Exposition, the Institute moved to its present Renaissance palace at Michigan and Adams.

Yet not quite, for it has often been enlarged, above ground and under ground and across the railroad tracks. Since 1925 it has embraced the Kenneth Sawyer Goodman Memorial Theater and School of Drama and much besides. Martin Ryerson and Charles L. Hutchinson (its president from 1882 to 1924) are the great names in its history. On their own responsibility, in Florence in 1890, they paid $200,000 for fifteen old masters—"corkers, every one," as Hutchinson told the reporters in characteristic Chicago style. This great-hearted Christian gentleman, son of the "Old Hutch" who ran the famous corner in wheat, was also interested in parks and playgrounds and acted as father-confessor to all Chicago. For him it was not enough to possess a picture like El Greco's *Assumption of the Virgin;* all Chicago must come to see it, and nobody ever surpassed him and his associates in making a city art-conscious and placing the support of an art museum upon the broadest possible basis. Now one of the four largest art museums in America, the Institute has a collection valued at more than $250,000,-000, a school embracing some six thousand students, ranging all the way from the elementary level to graduate work, and important libraries of art and architecture. Closed only on Christmas Day, it accommodates 1,300,000 visitors annually without charge. All in all, the bronze lions of Edward Kemeys (1894) have a right to look haughtily up and down the avenue, but they are gentle beasts at heart, as every child in Chicago knows, though nobody has ever succeeded in persauding one of them to look him in the eye.

The unmatched array of French paintings includes collections made by or named for Henry Field, Albert A. Munger, Mrs. Potter Palmer, Frederic Clay Bartlett, and others, and the George Inness room has been a glory as far back as anybody can remember. On the other hand, the plaster casts of Hasselberg's *The Snowdrop* and Chapu's *Joan of Arc at Domremy*, once prominently displayed inside the main entrance (they were so popular that the museum even sold small reproductions of them) have long since mysteriously disappeared; so has Bouguereau's painting, *The Bathers*, once one of the treasures of the town but now consigned to the dustbin out of consideration for the limitations of people who cannot run the risk of admiring anything which does not happen to be currently popular. One of the special attractions of the Art Institute during recent years has been the exquisite sixty-eight miniature rooms created by Mrs. James Ward Thorne, permitting a wider range of architectural interest and display than any museum could have either the money or the space to create full-scale and embodying an exquisite, diminutive beauty all their own.

The Chicago Natural History Museum has occupied its thirteen-acre building at the south end of Grant Park since 1921, when it moved over from the old Fine Arts Building. (It now entertains more visitors in a month than it then received in a year.) It embraces anthropology, geology, botany, and zoology. It has organized innumerable expeditions, among them that headed by Theodore Roosevelt, Jr. and Kermit Roosevelt in southern Asia, which brought back, among other things, the Marco Polo's sheep which every visitor to the museum has seen; it carries on endless important research and publishes its findings; and, like the Art Institute, it extends itself indefatigably into schools, libraries, reformatories, boys' clubs, etc.; nobody who wishes to learn about natural history is too humble to interest the museum. It was a child of the World's Columbian Exposition and one more evidence of the enormous interest in every branch of art and learning which the fair stimulated, and Marshall Field made his initial gift of $1,000,000 in the fair year. When he died in 1906, he left the museum $8,000,000—$4,000,000 toward the new building and $4,000,000 more toward endowment.

It may seem silly to make the point that the Natural History Museum is not an art museum; yet, as a matter of fact, it is hard for an aesthetically minded person to remember this, for the glorious Greek temple which it inhabits is of itself a great work of art, and what are we to say of such interior beauties as Herbert Haseltine's bronze and marble sculptures of British champion domestic animals? or again of one of the finest collections of gems and jewels in the world, including "Columbian gold ornaments, Egyptian and Etruscan jewelry, jewelry of the Greek and Roman periods in Egypt," and much besides, which are quite at home in the Department of Geology since gems are minerals? And who shall say that there is no art in the spectacular exhibits of men and animals against beautiful, lifelike reconstructions of their actual habitats? One might well go to Africa and come home again without having seen the animal wonders spread out before the eyes of every visitor to the museum in the magnificent "African Waterhole" exhibit which fills the whole south end of Hall 22. But whether one comes as a casual observer, interested primarily in these impressive and beautiful things, or, for that matter, in the two great African elephants, collected and mounted by Carl E. Akeley, which dominate Stanley Field Hall, and the immense skeletons of the dinosaurs, or whether one comes as a serious student desiring to make a systematic survey of the exhibits of Asiatic mammals, moon meteorites and minerals, Stone Age man, the archaeology of Egypt, or fossil plants and invertebrates, the museum will not let him down, though it does not pretend to have everything, and in view of what it has now compared to what it had when it moved into its already crowded huge building, who knows what wonders the future may have to offer?

Judged by actual attendance figures, the most popular museum in Chicago is the Museum of Science and Industry, which entertained over 2,760,000 people in 1962. If the Natural History Museum displays the resources of our world, then this museum shows what man has made and is making of them. On the central rotunda the visitor reads: SCIENCE DISCERNS THE LAWS OF NATURE—INDUSTRY APPLIES THEM TO THE NEEDS OF MAN. With this in mind, the Museum "endeavors to show the meaning of science translated by industry into terms of living, to show how the combination of science and industry produces the American way of life, to show the newest development as well as that which is historic." Firms may participate upon invitation, but they must keep up their exhibits, and they cannot use advertising slogans or give anything away. More than in any other museum, the spectator produces the show by pushing buttons or turning cranks; sometimes he himself becomes a part of the picture.

Some of it is pure science, but much of it is geared to those whose primary interest is in the application of science. Thus one may go down into a coal mine, inspect a captured German submarine, handle the throttle of a locomotive, watch baby chicks being hatched out, see a newspaper produced, walk on a moving rubber sidewalk of the future, or enter a gigantic model of a human heart and watch and hear its functioning. Nor has the Museum been fanatical about not crossing over the line which separates science from history or even art. Its possession of a five thousand-year-old chariot, supposed to be the oldest wheeled vehicle in existence, has its scientific aspect, but the "Yesterday's Main Street" exhibit is scientific only in the sense that the pictures shown in the nickelodeon are produced by electricity, and Colleen Moore's $500,000 Doll House, with its imaginative fairy lore, is no more scientific than the Thorne Rooms at the Art Institute; the making of both involved the use of mathematics, and that is all. The Museum has housed a Civil War Centennial display, a "Christmas Around the World" festival, and a "Miracle of Books" fair for girls and boys; there have even been outdoor concerts by the Chicago Chamber Orchestra.

I should like to write of Chicago museums at much greater length, but I have space to refer to only one more, the Chicago Historical Society, which was organized in 1856 and has occupied its present beautiful building in Lincoln Park since 1932. Originally the Society confined itself to memorabilia of Chicago and the Midwest; the emphasis is still here, but of late years the scope has widened. It is interesting to remember that its officers were alert enough to make a bid for the Lincoln Papers as far back as 1882, but Robert Lincoln did not then think there was anything of sufficient interest or importance to justify preservation!

Nevertheless, Lincoln is all over the museum; there are reproductions of the cabin he was born in, his parlor in Springfield, and the bedroom in the Petersen house in which he died, to say nothing of the twenty really beautiful dioramas, showing scenes and events in his life, which are certainly one of the more creditable monuments of the WPA. Another series of dioramas shows representative Chicago scenes, beginning with the Greenville Treaty of 1795, and including both the Fire and the World's Columbian Exposition; by turning a switch the visitor can see the Court of Honor by night or by day.

There are Spanish and French Exploration rooms, a reproduction of Paul Revere's house in Boston, and exhibits illustrating many periods in Chicago and national history. The Fort Dearborn Massacre monument, formerly on the site of the slaughter, has now been moved into the museum for safekeeping. And, like all good modern museums, the Society carries on a program of research, publication, and extension.

Only once do the authorities seem to have allowed a deplorable pusillanimity to stand in the way of their securing a valuable relic. In 1943, Sally Rand offered the fans she had used in her dances at the Century of Progress Exposition, and the current director, L. H. Shattuck, accepted with appropriate gratitude, only to be overruled by the Board of Trustees, which stuffily found the articles in question of insufficient "historical interest to warrant their acceptance by a museum," so that Miss Rand, all ready to go out and make the presentation, was stopped dead in her tracks. She was very angry, and who could blame her? But perhaps she felt better after the Decatur *Herald* had demonstrated that the decision was, after all, inevitable. "It is true, of course," wrote David V. Felts, "that nobody was interested in seeing Sally's fans, even in 1933. They tried to see Sally and the fans were always in the way."

8

Today and Tomorrow

Wᴴᴇɴ I think back to my Chicago childhood, two contrasted pictures come before my mind. Next door to the house in which we lived was a vacant lot, and every spring this would burst out into a gorgeous bloom of dandelions. It was the brilliant yellow of the dandelion blossoms against the equally vivid green of the grass that I found so overwhelming, a lesson in color almost too powerful to be borne.

Just about the same time of the year the makers of Zu Zu Ginger Snaps used to get out a new set of posters, calling attention to their wares with gorgeously colored pictures of the clowns who were their principal advertising device, and these they would plaster all over the Elevated stations. If anybody had given me one to take home, I should have been as enthralled as I could be today with a Leonardo.

I am aware that it is not proper to admire the dandelion, though I have always suspected that if it had to be cultivated, it might be admired more. And such painters as Van Gogh and Gauguin and Bakst have now taught us that the primary colors can be more "aesthetic" than it was once the fashion to believe. But never mind that. Let the dandelions and the posters both be "vulgar." It is tragic never to learn to admire anything but vulgar things, but it is also tragic to outgrow them completely, for you cannot spend your whole life in the presence of either great art or supreme beauty, and if you only come alive in their presence, you are going to be dead much of the time. I could have had the dandelions in the country but not the clowns on the Elevated platforms; in Chicago I had both. And Chicago was the right place to relish them, for it is recorded that in the early days of Lincoln Park there was one who thought there should be wildlife in the park; so he went east and came back with—English sparrows!

I have said that there is no use trying to be neutral about Chicago. What I should think of her if I were to approach her now for the first time, I have no way to tell. As a youngster I used to walk her streets grateful to God that my lot had been cast with her rather than elsewhere, and I still find Michigan Avenue between the Blackstone and the Water Tower far more exciting than any street in New York. Up to now my life has been very symmetrical geographically speaking. I was born in Chicago and lived there until I was twenty-five. Then I went to Seattle to teach in the University of Washington, where I remained eighteen years. I returned to Chicago to teach four years at Illinois Institute of Technology and to live in Evanston. My next move was to Boston University, and when I have taught there exactly eighteen years, I shall have reached the normal retirement age. To make symmetry perfect, it would only be necessary at this point to return to the Chicago area and live there twenty-five years more, which would bring me to the very reasonable age of ninety.

I shall not do it, for though Chicago excited me as much as ever the last time I visited there, I also felt very strongly that I did not desire to put in any more hours of my life riding on the Elevated. The truth of the matter is that I have fallen out of love with all cities and that the New England countryside has captured me. When retirement time comes, I shall head north, only taking care to keep within hailing distance of the Boston area libraries. So this book turns out after all to be a love letter to mother from an unfaithful son. But as Henry Adams says, "All children wander with the truant Time."

But what of her future, which should be more interesting to the reader of this book than mine? It is a part of the future of the country and of the world, and there are both lights and shadows in the crystal ball which cannot be spelled out here. There are great building enterprises under way in Chicago; there is a great Chicago Plan to be completed— and enlarged beyond anything its framers dreamed of. She also has terrible problems to face: cowards would call them insoluble problems. Occasioned by technological change, accentuated by population shifts, they include illiteracy (one survey showed 50.7 per cent of Chicago's jobless, able-bodied reliefers illiterate, which is a rate five times the national average), illegitimacy, race conflict, and crime. In March, 1962, the Board of Education undertook an adult education all-out attack on illiteracy which has already paid amazing dividends, but the most encouraging thing about it is not the number of people it has taken off relief but the evidence it has afforded that even those whom Chicago has found at the bottom of the social pyramid, or has cast there, have not yet given themselves up as a bad job.

As I have said before, there is no completely satisfactory purely human answer to any human problem, but people are people, no matter where they come from or what they look like. I can remember when some of those who have since proved themselves among Chicago's most valuable assets belonged to groups who were regarded by the old-timers as certain to destroy everything that the founding fathers had created. I see no reason to doubt that the same play will be produced again with a fresh cast. And once more I expect the production to be enthralling.

—————— *Selected Bibliography* ——————

O<small>NLY</small> a few of the works consulted in preparing this book can be listed here. The standard history of Chicago, replacing earlier works, is now Bessie Louise Pierce, *A History of Chicago* (Knopf, 1937, 1940, 1957). Unfortunately the third volume reaches only to 1893. See also the same author's *As Others See Chicago: Impressions of Visitors, 1673–1933* (University of Chicago Press, 1933). Milo M. Quaife, *Chicago and the Old Northwest 1673–1835* (Chicago, 1913) is the fullest account of the early period, but his *Checagou: From Indian Wigwam to Modern City, 1673–1835* (Chicago, 1933) is more interesting reading for the general reader.

Among the following general books about Chicago, I have starred those which I found most useful: Robert Shackleton, *The Book of Chicago* (Penn, 1929); William H. Hudson, ed., *Chicago, A History and a Forecast* (Chicago Association of Commerce, 1921); John Drury, *Chicago in Seven Days* (McBride, 1928); *Lloyd Lewis and Henry Justin Smith, *Chicago: The History of its Reputation* (Harcourt, 1929); *Charles E. Merriam, *Chicago: A More Intimate View of Urban Politics* (Macmillan, 1929); Henry R. Hamilton, *The Epic of Chicago* (Willett, Clark, 1932); Edgar Lee Masters, *The Tale of Chicago* (Putnam, 1933); H. J. Smith, *Chicago's Great Century, 1833–1933*

(Chicago, Consolidated Publishers, 1933); *Ernest Poole, *Giants Gone* (Whittlesey House, 1943); Dorsha B. Hayes, *Chicago, Crossroads of American Enterprise* (Messner, 1944); *Wayne Andrews, *Battle for Chicago* (Harcourt, 1946); Evelyn F. Carlson, *A Great City and State* (Chicago, King Company, 1947); *Emmett Dedmon, *Fabulous Chicago* (Random House, 1953); *Herman Kogan and Lloyd Wendt, *Chicago: A Pictorial History* (Dutton, 1958).

H. C. Chatfield-Taylor, *Chicago* (Houghton Mifflin, 1917) is a delightful essay, glorified by the beautiful illustrations of Lester G. Hornby, finely reproduced, and E. H. Suydam's fine pictures add to the value of H. J. Smith, *Chicago, A Portrait* (Century, 1931). See also Chatfield-Taylor, *Cities of Many Men* (Houghton Mifflin, 1925); among countless other books of reminiscences are Louise de Koven Bowen, *Growing Up with a City* (Macmillan, 1926); Ralph Fletcher Seymour, *Some Went This Way* (Chicago, Seymour, 1945); Robert J. Casey, *Chicago Medium Rare* (Bobbs-Merrill, 1952); Arthur Meeker, *Chicago, With Love* (Knopf, 1955); Robert Hardy Andrews, *A Corner of Chicago* (Little, Brown, 1963). For contemporary Chicago, see A. J. Liebling, *Chicago, The Second City* (Knopf, 1952); Martha Bennett King, *The Key to Chicago* (Lippincott, 1961); Irv Kupcinet, *Kup's Chicago* (World, 1962). Good modern pictorials are Arthur Haug and Robert Cromie, *Chicago* (Ziff-Davis, 1948); Fred Korth, *The Chicago Book* (Chicago, Korth, 1949).

The best account of the Fire is Robert Cromie, *The Great Chicago Fire* (McGraw-Hill, 1958). Harry Hansen wrote *The Chicago* in the "Rivers of America" series (Farrar and Rinehart, 1942). For the World's Columbian Exposition, see Hubert H. Bancroft, *The Book of the Fair*

(Chicago and San Francisco, The Bancroft Company, 1893). The best book on merchandising is the history of Marshall Field's by Lloyd Wendt and Herman Kogan, *Give the Lady What She Wants!* (Rand McNally, 1952). For the underworld see the same authors, *Lords of the Levee* (Bobbs-Merrill, 1943) and Herbert Asbury's more lurid *Gem of the Prairie* (Knopf, 1940).

On literature there are two valuable unpublished University of Chicago Ph.D. dissertations: Lennox Bouton Grey "Chicago and 'The Great American Novel': A Critical Approach to the American Epic" (1925) and Hugh Dalziel Duncan, "Chicago as a Literary Center: Social Factors Influencing Chicago Literary Institutions from 1865 to 1920" (1948). See also Bernard Duffey, *The Chicago Renaissance in American Letters* (Michigan State College Press, 1954). Sidney Kramer, *A History of Stone & Kimball and Herbert S. Stone and Co. . . .* (Chicago, 1940) is delightful in text and picture. Albert Halper, *This is Chicago* (Holt, 1952) is an anthology of fiction and nonfiction about Chicago. John J. McPhaul, *Deadlines and Monkeyshines* (Prentice-Hall, 1962) is a lively book about Chicago journalism. The official history of the *Tribune*, Philip Kinsley, *The Chicago Tribune: Its First Hundred Years* (Vol. I, Knopf, 1943; Vols. II, III, Chicago Tribune, 1945, 1946) was unfortunately abandoned at the year 1900. For the *Daily News*, see Charles H. Dennis, *Victor Lawson: His Time and His Work* (Chicago, 1935). For architecture, see Wayne Andrews, *Architecture, Ambition, and Americans* (Harper, 1955). Edward C. Moore covers opera to 1929 in *Forty Years of Opera in Chicago* (Liveright, 1930). Paul M. Angle, *The Chicago Historical Society, 1856–1956: An Unconventional Chronicle* (Rand McNally, 1956) is lively and lavishly illustrated.

There is no space available to list biographies of the many men and women referred to in these pages, but most of them are in the *Dictionary of American Biography*, and the reader who looks them up there will find many of the important biographical works listed.

174

THE CENTERS OF CIVILIZATION SERIES, of which this volume is the thirteenth is intended to include accounts of the great cities of the world during particular periods of their flowering, from ancient times to the present. The following list is complete as of the date of publication of this volume.